TRANSFORMATIVE MANAGEMENT EDUCATION

Due to the recent global financial crises, academic business schools have come in for much criticism, having, in the eyes of the public, failed in their responsibility to society by teaching future managers only how to increase their personal gain without any consideration as to the social and cultural consequences of their actions. Realising that there is a pressing need to innovate their educational offers accordingly, business schools are beginning to turn to the humanities and social sciences to improve on the understanding and thus the teaching of management.

This book is the result of an empirical study conducted at eight academic business schools that either already practise or are beginning to practise linking management education to the humanities and social sciences. Gathered mostly in interviews our research team conducted during site visits to these schools, the material presented shows three major fields of concern: how to shift the focus from instrumental to transformative learning, how to reframe the concept of disciplinary subject matter towards a more relational understanding of knowledge—especially in the light of the impact digitalisation is having on education—and how to address the organisational, as well as the political consequences of management education turning towards the inclusion of the humanities and social sciences strategically. The findings indicate that the humanities and social sciences indeed offer knowledge which can significantly help management education with meeting the challenges of the twenty-first century.

Innovating management education by making it part of its programme portfolios proves a challenge in and of itself in the face of a university system which still determinedly clings to disciplinary segregation. Reforming management education towards an engagement with fields of knowledge traditionally at best ignored and at worst vilified as being completely useless in the "real world" may therefore place academic business schools at the forefront of a movement that is beginning to reshape the educational landscape as a whole. This book will be of value to researchers, academics and students in the fields of business, management studies, organisational studies and education studies.

Ulrike Landfester is a Professor of German Language and Literature at University of St. Gallen, Switzerland.

Jörg Metelmann is Associate Professor of Culture and Media Studies at the University of St. Gallen, Switzerland.

Routledge Advances in Management and Business Studies

For more information about this series, please visit www.routledge.com/series/SE0305

TRANSFORMATIVE MANAGEMENT EDUCATION

The Role of the Humanities and Social Sciences

Ulrike Landfester and Jörg Metelmann
in collaboration with Nicolaj Tofte Brenneche
and Queralt Prat-i-Pubill

Routledge
Taylor & Francis Group

NEW YORK AND LONDON

First published 2019
by Routledge
52 Vanderbilt Avenue, New York, NY 10017

and by Routledge
2 Park Square, Milton Park, Abingdon, Oxon, OX14 4RN

Routledge is an imprint of the Taylor & Francis Group, an informa business

© 2019 Taylor & Francis

The right of Ulrike Landfester and Jörg Metelmann to be identified
as authors of this work has been asserted by them in accordance with
sections 77 and 78 of the Copyright, Designs and Patents Act 1988.

Library of Congress Cataloging-in-Publication Data
Names: Landfester, Ulrike, 1962– author. | Metelmann, Jèorg, author.
Title: Transformative management education : the role of the humanities
    and social sciences / Ulrike Landfester and Jèorg Metelmann ; in
    collaboration with Nicolaj Tofte Brenneche and Queralt Prat-i-Pubill.
Description: New York, NY : Routledge, 2019. | Series: Routledge
    advances in management and business studies | Includes bibliographical
    references.
Identifiers: LCCN 2018044799 | ISBN 9780367076733 (hardback) |
    ISBN 9780367076740 (pbk.) | ISBN 9780429022005 (ebook)
Subjects: LCSH: Management—Study and teaching (Higher) | Business
    education. | Humanities—Study and teaching. | Social sciences—
    Study and teaching. | Transformative learning.
Classification: LCC HD30.4 .L358 2019 | DDC 658.0071/1—dc23
LC record available at https://lccn.loc.gov/2018044799

ISBN: 9780367076733 (hbk)
ISBN: 9780367076740 (pbk)
ISBN: 9780429022005 (ebk)

Typeset in Bembo
by Apex CoVantage, LLC

MIX
Paper from
responsible sources
FSC
www.fsc.org   FSC® C013056

Printed and bound in Great Britain by
TJ International Ltd, Padstow, Cornwall

CONTENTS

FOREWORD

This book is that *rara avis*, a stirring, even inspiring report. There are three major features that make it worth reading. First, because as research the book breaks new ground, for anyone interested in the preparation of tomorrow's business professionals, and the organisations that educate them, the findings are revealing and therefore interesting in themselves; second, because the authors have used their empirical findings to formulate and develop a powerful, core theoretical argument for moving management programmes towards what they call transformative education; and, third, because the report advances a compelling narrative that articulates the need for and possibility of a movement to reshape management learning in ways that hold significance for the whole enterprise of higher education, both in Europe and elsewhere.

The authors write as a team of researchers who have spent several years visiting and interviewing instructors and academic leaders at seven European business schools as well as the Singapore Management University. They chose these organisational sites for their field study because all describe their management programmes as intentionally aiming to integrate business disciplines with other areas of the arts and sciences, especially those the report calls 'humanities'. The authors report a rising groundswell of opinion among the management faculty with whom they spoke that today's increasingly challenging and unstable business environment demands that graduates of management programmes be equipped with more than a fixed 'tool kit' of technical skills. Today's students need more than that. The authors call this something more 'transformative education'. To prosper in business careers, they argue, students will also have to know how to keep learning, how to revise their perspective on the world and themselves and how to think imaginatively yet responsibly as business professionals.

Such a programme is far from academic business as usual. Rather, it intentionally aims to develop students' ability to learn how to draw upon the whole range of knowledge and modes of thinking relevant to today's business context. At the core of this model of learning is what the authors call interdisciplinary integration. As they explain this concept, the authors lead the reader to understand why the perspectives of 'the humanities'—by which they mean both fields such as psychology and sociology, that are usually called social sciences, as well as disciplines like philosophy, history and literature—are essential to management learning. The humanities, understood in this broad sense, provide the conceptual matrix for understanding the contexts and motivations within which business situations arise and in which technical skills must be deployed. They also provide models and possibilities for making personal sense of what is encountered as part of preparing for a career in business. A key purpose of the report is to articulate what this insight means for management learning practices, including curricular content and the structure of management programmes.

A particular strength of the report is that it does not simply make its argument on the theoretical level, impressive as its rationale turns out to be. That is, it provides inspiration as well as information about transformative education for management. The report describes several versions of such interdisciplinary, integrative management education as well as how some of those involved in such learning practices understand what they are doing. Balancing the positive examples with critical commentary, the authors also analyse the limitations that current organisational structures in many business schools place on changing what they describe as an all-too-common reliance on mere information transfer into the more engaging and dynamic forms of management learning they advocate. In addition, they take up the important question of how such transformative learning is to be assessed—while noting the powerful influence that competitive ranking and accreditation standards exert on those responsible for management programmes.

But the report does not leave the issue there, in the matter of fact. Instead, the authors close with a well-considered argument for why the kind of reshaping of management education which they advocate—and which their research shows to be already underway—needs fuller articulation in order to take the still largely inchoate movement to a next level of organisation. They call for a bold effort: to 'rebrand' management training as transformational education of the type they advocate. As a cooperative effort among schools across disparate national contexts, such a movement has the potential not only to enhance student learning and add value for graduates' careers but also to upgrade the quality and prestige of management programmes both in Europe and beyond.

The Findings

From their visits to the eight business schools—Copenhagen Business School; Escola Superior d'Administració i Direcció d'Empreses (ESADE), Barcelona; Koç University, Istanbul; Lancaster University Management School; Stockholm School of Economics; University of St. Gallen; Aalto University School of Business;

Singapore Management University—and scores of interviews during the academic years 2014 and 2015, as well as a wide-ranging review of the research literature, the authors are able to provide an overview of how management faculty across Europe understand their students, their educational aims and their situation as educators. The report's middle chapters give new insight by illustrating generalisations with many often piquant quotations, through which the interviewees speak for themselves. In addition, these chapters also locate individual views within larger institutional contexts of both the business schools or operation universities and the national educational systems in which they are embedded. This provides a rich and nuanced view of the various debates 'on the ground' between defenders of programmes based exclusively on the established business disciplines versus advocates of using the humanities as an integrative matrix to enable students to learn technical business skills while developing the mind-set of self-directed business professionals.

From their data, the authors are able to provide insight into several common problems. For example, their interviews reveal a widespread perception among management faculty that their students arrive n higher education with what the authors call an instrumental mind-set. This means that students tend to judge their programmes and courses primarily for their potential 'cash value' and how the students imagine (often on the basis of hearsay rather than actual knowledge) their learning will help them gain lucrative employment in the shortest time. Unfortunately, the researchers show, this attitude is often reinforced rather than disputed by the organisational structure and operation of many management programmes. The result is to short-change the students by avoiding a key educational responsibility to challenge students' ignorance while leading them towards a wider perspective.

Again, the report sheds light on the too-facile and limiting equation of humanistic learning in management with courses of business ethics. This view is also widespread among business faculty, one sometimes reinforced by humanities faculty themselves when, in an effort to legitimate their place in management education, they present their disciplines as 'rescuing' business education from amorality by proposing the high road of moral integrity. Given the arrogance easily associated with this strategy for legitimating humanistic learning, the consequence is too often a subtle or not-so-subtle resistance to pleas to introduce more humanities into the curriculum. Here, one of the report's contributions is to show how the pre-existing structural division of management education by intellectual discipline strengthens the opposition to further integration of humanistic learning into the curriculum.

The Theoretical Core Argument

The authors' most original contribution may lie in their framing of the larger dialogue about improving undergraduate management education. They put forward a concept they call transformative education as the best perspective within which to understand both the strengths and the deficiencies which their field research has uncovered. It is this concept that justifies the authors' urging of the extra efforts that will be needed to move management education forward to a broader and, they insist, more effective 'brand' of higher education.

The typical approach to increased demands for higher standards in management education, in Europe as in North America, has been additive. That is, new elements are added to an existing curriculum of study, perhaps with some amendments to forms of teaching and learning, but still keeping sharp distinctions between forms of inquiry and matters of content based in distinct intellectual disciplines. The educational assumption underlying this strategy, as the report notes, is that education is in its essence the packaging and transmission of various kinds of information and particular technical skills that students are imagined to somehow store away for later use. Separate bits of knowledge, and discreet packages of skills, are simply added to one another to produce a finished educational product. For many in the business schools, this seems common sense.

However, as the report emphasises, decades of research on how learning actually takes place have shown this 'common sense' to be false. Learning that lasts is not additive. It is not primarily the acquiring and storing of information and processing skills. Rather, it is a matter of what learning psychology has described as the making of meaning. Content, that is, becomes important—is learned in the sense of becoming part of the learner's habits of mind and disposition only as it becomes integrated and consolidated with the learner's sense of self and orientation to the world. And, as the literature on learning makes clear, this is a developmental process that requires the careful design of educational experiences that spur growth in learners' capacities to understand the world and themselves. Learning thus emerges as an engaged process in which the learner's perspectives change and grow as learning advances. One does not complete a genuine process of learning as the same person who began it.

Transformative learning calls attention to this priority of meaning-making over the processing of information. It is concerned with cultivating the motivation to learn as well as developing techniques to foster learning as an ongoing, lifelong process. The particular value of the humanities, as the report articulates it, is that these fields provide ways to facilitate the all-important making of meaning that underlies real learning. But, going further, transformative education means not just adding humanities content or skills to an already existing set of business content and skills, but instead insists upon genuinely integrating the perspectives currently often separated into windowless disciplinary contexts. Students are too rarely provided with the contexts, models, intellectual tools and opportunities for experiment with critical feedback that are necessary to realise the potential of integrating humanities with business. In response, this report provides a clear account of the how as well as the why of such an integrated approach to management learning.

What Makes the Argument Compelling

Finally, what makes the argument of *Transformative Management Education: The Role of the Humanities and Social Sciences* compelling reading is its form. The report takes the reader into a narrative of struggle and seeks to enlist the reader as a supporter and participant in that struggle. The problem underlying the current state of mainstream management education, say the report's authors, which is institutionally embodied in the limitations of the 'additive' curriculum, is the extreme specialisation of the university's disciplinary system; hence, the authors' central point that, in order to produce better business professionals, management education must be grounded in interdisciplinary integration. Much of the report is devoted to explaining what this means and how it might be done, including compelling examples. But this will require struggle to overcome existing obstacles as well as to convince and enlist a critical mass of stakeholders in management education.

To motivate this struggle, the authors place their findings, their recommendations and their core theory within an agonistic narrative, which enables the reader to see, perhaps for the first time, the issues in their proper proportions. The source of the woes afflicting contemporary management education arises from the historical devolution of the idea of modern higher education itself. As first conceived at the beginning of the nineteenth century by Wilhelm von Humboldt and institutionalised in the first modern university at Berlin, the university was to educate citizens for an emerging cosmopolitan world by instilling the Enlightenment's ethos of curiosity, learning and research as a shared enterprise directed towards the general welfare.

In this founding vision, learning, scholarship and research were perceived as expressions of a human rationality which, as such, already embodied a moral aim at the common good. However, as knowledge became more complex, and social reality more complicated, the research function became ever more specialised and, with it, came the division of teaching and learning into barely communicating spheres. The university's larger, cohesive aims were gradually eclipsed. When business entered higher education, first in the USA and then later in Europe and elsewhere, it emulated this disciplinary drive. The consequences have, however, been quite mixed, as the report documents, so that disciplinary specialisation has come to retard as well as advance learning. Today, following the Great Recession of 2008 and the instability it spread throughout the interconnected global society, an inflection point has arrived. As demands on both business organisations and higher education mount, retrieving Humboldt's vision in a twenty-first century form promises to rekindle hopes that the university might yet help inspire a more just and humane future. Advancing that cause through recasting the norms of management education is the large cause for which the report seeks to enlist its readers' loyalty. To a remarkable extent, it succeeds.

William M. Sullivan

1

INTRODUCTION

"There Is Something About the Humanities . . .": Transformative Management Education Meets the Humanities and Social Sciences

"There is something about the humanities . . .": again and again, we heard this sentence when researching the material for this report. In the overall context of the interviews we conducted at eight business schools which engage in the integration of the humanities and social sciences into management education, this sentence became something of a discursive icon, representing both the hopes tied to such integrational endeavours and the problems coming with them. There is something in the humanities—of that nearly all our interviewees were certain—something which was perceived by them to promise a positive influence on management education. However, rarely was the sentence said with the full conviction of having identified a problem and found a solution which now simply needed to be implemented; rather, it always seemed to beg more questions than it answered. Yes, there is something in the humanities—but what precisely is that? And how can business schools practically go about making it available to management students?

In the course of our research, we found that, however difficult it might seem to articulate concrete answers to these questions, discussing them showed one link between management education and the humanities and social sciences, which was perceived if not explicitly to offer, then at least to lead, towards answers: a link which became more clearly visible with each stage of our project. Our book's title, *Transformative Management Education: The Role of the Humanities and Social Sciences*, showcases this link. All the business schools that we researched were working towards changing management education, away from merely providing students with applicable technical skills in specialised areas, into an educational experience which would transform students holistically, through enhancing their understanding of and interaction with the social, economic and cultural contexts of management—and at all of those schools, the humanities and social sciences were perceived to play an important role in this endeavour.

The concept of transformative education has significantly gained impact on adult education ever since the American sociologist Jack Mezirow started to develop and propagate the idea in the 1970s (Mezirow, 1978). While he consistently used the term 'transformative learning' to encode his theory of adult education, we, it will be noted, use the term 'transformative education', which was introduced into the field later by Robert Boyd (Boyd & Myers, 1988; Boyd, 1991), as this seems to us the more generally applicable term. Whether the differences between Mezirow's, Boyd's and indeed Paulo Freire's (Freire, 1970) approaches to transformational education are as incisive as Edward W. Taylor, in his comparative study of those three approaches (Taylor, 1998), has made out remains to be seen. On our part, we judge these three contributions to transformative education to be made in a similar spirit, however stringently Mezirow emphasises critical rationality as the mainstay of the transformational process, while Boyd advocates the inclusion of emotional responses along psychological lines to ensure holistic individuation, and Freire sees transformational education as a means to the end of changing society as a whole (Freire, 1970); the latter is in fact listed by Mezirow as one of the most important inspirations on his way to transformation theory. In the end, all three aspects are tied up with each other in transformative management education, as will be seen from the results of our field study.

In a dialogue on transformative learning that Mezirow conducted with John Dirkx, the results of which were published in 2006, Mezirow presented what perhaps is his most clear-cut definition of transformative learning yet:

> This rational process of learning within awareness is a metacognitive application of critical thinking that transforms an acquired frame of reference—a mind-set or world-view of orienting assumptions and expectations involving values, beliefs and concepts—by assessing its epistemic assumptions.
>
> *(Cranton, 2006, p. 124)*

Basically, this means that transformative education is meant to make students aware of the fact that, long before entering the realm of adult education, the frames of reference they bring to their studies, far from mirroring unshakeable truths about reality, in fact are concepts constructed by social and cultural norms. The potential for transformation mobilised by the process of learning lies in their realising this, analysing the agenda coming with those norms and consequently being able actively to pursue what Mezirow called "perspective transformation" (Mezirow, 1981, p. 3).

In this context, Mezirow explicitly pointed to the humanities and social sciences. Defining "learning as transformation" (Mezirow et al., 2000), he drew on Jürgen Habermas' classifying of human knowledge according to the three categories of instrumental, communicative and emancipatory knowledge (Habermas, 1971). While Mezirow acknowledged that instrumental knowledge was certainly necessary to enable students to meet the technical demands of the labour market, he argued that the growing complexity of reality also demanded improvements in how communicative and emancipatory knowledge was imparted to students, claiming that this needed the hermeneutical approach applied by the humanities and social sciences:

> The historical-hermeneutic disciplines differ from the empirical-analytic sciences in the "content" studied, methods of inquiry and criteria for assessing alternative interpretations. They include descriptive social science, history, aesthetics, legal, ethnographic, literary and other studies interpreting the meaning of communicative experience.
>
> *(Mezirow, 1981, p. 5)*

thus laying the foundations for the acquisition of emancipatory knowledge through critical thinking and ultimately critical self-reflection.

While our interviewees' statements on this matter on the whole ran along the lines that Mezirow sketched out, these statements also show that, at business schools going for the integration of the humanities and social sciences, the motivation to do so is informed by two major considerations. One is specific to business schools, namely the still-smarting memory of the global financial crises during recent decades, which resulted in so much acrid societal criticism of the institutions responsible for producing the managers who had, if perhaps not actively promoted, at least spectacularly failed in averting those crises. The second and more generally applicable consideration is the growing consciousness that the working world for which the school's graduates were being prepared would be a VUCA world, as the famous Harvard acronym has it (that is, a world characterised by Volatility, Uncertainty, Complexity and Ambiguity), the demands of which were not, or at least not satisfactorily, being met by traditional management education. And as the humanities and social sciences are perceived to be the academic disciplines most concerned with dealing with the volatility of meaning, the uncertainty of how present technological and political developments may influence the world's future, the complexity of the human mind and its interaction with its environment, as well as the ambiguities encountered in intercultural communication; they are the disciplines believed to be uniquely qualified to prepare future managers and entrepreneurs for handling these phenomena.

Neither the awareness of the need to rethink management education in the light of its impact on society and of the issues suggested by the VUCA acronym, nor the idea that the humanities and social sciences should be called upon to contribute are new to the ongoing debate about academic management education. In 1959, the report on management education authored by Robert Aaron Gordon and James Edwin Howell stated decisively that

> [e]ducation for business must be a dynamic thing, sensitive both to the changing character of business itself and to the advances in the fields of

knowledge on which an understanding of business should be based. The need for experimentation and for keeping up with and applying new knowledge never ends.

(Gordon & Howell, 1959, p. 8)

Gordon and Howell recommend equally decisively that students, alongside their professional education, should also be offered a general education in non-business disciplines including the humanities and social sciences, to the extent of 60% of their overall course load (1959, pp. 152–53).

Since then, the questions of where exactly such integrated education should lead and what it should entail, though, have been and still are being discussed from rather widely varying points of view. The most prominent among recent contributions to this debate, undoubtedly, is the Carnegie report *Rethinking Undergraduate Business Education* (Colby et al., 2011), published in 2011, which focuses mainly on the prevention of another international economic meltdown, like the one engendered by the financial crises, by improving on the morals of future managers through the humanities and social sciences (or, as the US academic tradition has it, the liberal arts). However, if we compare the approach to integrating the humanities and social sciences into management education in the late 1950s as represented by Gordon's and Howell's *Higher Education for Business* to the approach chosen by the authors of the Carnegie report of 2011, we see a rather significant difference. Gordon and Howell list business ethics among the skills to be taught to management students as a necessity, remarking dryly that "[i]n most schools, emphasis on the development of ethical standards and a sense of social responsibility does not go much beyond the statement in the official bulletin" (1959, p. 45). They do not, however, link this directly to the humanities and social sciences; the role of the latter in their view is mainly to provide for linguistic competence (that is, improving writing and rhetorical skills) as well as historical, sociological and intercultural communication competence. The Carnegie report, on the other hand, argues for the contribution of the humanities and social sciences to management education mainly on the grounds that they should help to transform management students into better—i.e. more responsible and socially aware human beings, given that the morality of management studies' graduates, by the first decade of the twenty-first century, had obviously become a serious concern in its own right.

The point of view that the contribution of the humanities and social sciences is recognised mainly in the area of students' moral improvement mirrors a consensus that is found in nearly all recent reports on the future of management education and that is brought up in many of the interviews we conducted as well. Further questioning, however, as will be seen, elicited the fact that this consensus, at least among our interviewees, was not due to the sincere conviction that morals were indeed what the humanities and social sciences were all about. Instead, as we came to realise, there are two key factors shaping this perception: firstly, business ethics are the one interface between the humanities and management education which has been accepted into the mainstream of the latter. Therefore, the association with morality offers a convenient handle with which to describe the humanities' contributions to management education, whereas, secondly, the conceptualising and thus the strategic translation of those contributions into other terms as easily available as the concept of morals is still conspicuously missing from academic discourse, not only on the part of management education but also—or even mainly—on the part of the humanities and social sciences themselves. Thus, when the latter's contribution is narrowed down to moral improvement, this indicates a problem in academic interdisciplinary communication which, it will be seen, in turn indicates a problem in the disciplinary system of the Humboldtian university, in the end begging the question as to whether this system is adequate to sustaining the future of management education.

The Point of Departure: From the Carnegie Report of 2011 to the "Humanities' Business" Research Project

At the time when we started to work on the research for this report, none of the conclusions from our later findings which we hinted at in the previous paragraph were even faintly in evidence. Our point of entry into the field of reporting on the development of management education was determined by the combination of two factors, one being the appearance of the Carnegie report of 2011, the other being the fact that the University of St. Gallen (HSG) has been practising the integration of the humanities and social sciences into management education from the time of its foundation in 1898 in one way or another, the extent and practice of such integration having gone through multiple stages of emergence but always remaining an integral part of the university's strategic discourse. As both of this report's authors are part of the School of Humanities and Social Sciences (SHSS) which is responsible for what at HSG is called the Contextual Studies programme, currently allowing (or from a different perspective, obliging) all students to acquire 25% of their credit points in this programme, we were electrified by the strong arguments made by the Carnegie report's authors in favour of a liberal arts general education, especially as the HSG Presidency had just charged SHSS with conducting a thorough reform of contextual studies.

To support the reform process, the Presidency in 2013 launched a research project which was to link the reform with the international debate on the future of management education and to provide empirical research into best practices in how business schools were integrating the humanities and social sciences into their curricula. The two persons charged with conducting the project were Ulrike Landfester, professor of German language and literature at SHSS and currently the university's vice-president for external relations, as chair, and Jörg Metelmann, associate professor of culture and media studies at SHSS, programme director of the leadership skills curriculum in contextual studies and academic director of the coaching programme on the assessment level. We dubbed it the "humanities' business" project, having devised for it the self-explanatory motto "Humanity's business is the humanities' business", and we recruited two additional researchers with the funding provided by the president: Dr. Nicolaj Tofte Brenneche, a graduate in philosophy and business studies from Copenhagen Business School, and Dr. Queralt Prat-i-Pubill, who graduated from ESADE, Barcelona, and has a mixed academic and industrial background, combining doctoral research into creativity with several years' working experience in the global financial sector and as a start-up entrepreneur in media innovation.

Working our collective way through the many contributions to the ongoing debate about management education to decide on our own approach, our team found that there is an exhilarating richness of literature on the historical evolution, institutional frameworks and learning purposes of business schools' management education programmes. However, there were two aspects which struck us as especially significant for the orientation of our research. First, most of the reports on management education that we read are mainly concerned with well-established educational paradigms and seldom take pioneering or experimental practices into account. At the same time, even empirically based studies which advocate the integration of the humanities and social sciences into management education (e.g. Starkey & Tempest, 2008; Harney & Thomas, 2013; Thomas et al., 2014) offer little, if any information on how this is achieved practically.

There are, however, some recently published exceptions to which our work owes much information as well as inspiration. One is *Shaping the Future of Business Education: Relevance, Rigor, and Life Preparation*, edited by Gordon M. Hardy and Daniel L. Everett in 2013, which in some ways can be read as a sequel to the Carnegie report from 2011. The book covers the American approach to integrating the humanities and social sciences—in the USA, mostly referred to as the liberal arts—into business education and vice versa, placing its subject into the broad historical and institutional context of higher education. Another book which needs to be mentioned here is *Integrative Approaches to Sustainable Development at University Level: Making the Links*, edited by Walter Leal Filho et al. in 2015, a global collection of inspiring case studies on how to integrate education in sustainability into higher education. Though this book focuses on the issue of sustainability and hardly mentions the humanities and social sciences at all, as well as being not primarily about business schools but universities in general, the topics addressed by the contributors are basically the same as those on which business schools integrating the humanities and social sciences into management education are working, especially concerning the shift from instrumental to transformative education by means of interdisciplinary integration. The *Routledge Companion to Reinventing Management Education*, edited by Chris Steyaert et al. in 2016, on the other hand, explicitly focuses on the integration of the humanities and social sciences into management education, offering, like Leal Filho et al. (2015), a rich collection of case studies on teaching practices as well as on strategic and operational framings, in a manner similar to that of Hardy and Everett (2013). Taken together, those books encouragingly show that current research has begun to take up transformative education with a seriousness that promises well for the latter's institutional future.

The second aspect which guided the orientation of our research was that, generally, literature on management education shows a strong tendency to concentrate on the Anglo-American business school community, specifically on US business schools and their traditions. This tendency certainly makes sense in view of how strong this community is in both supplying and researching management education; however, the deductions and arguments of these authors are not easily transferable into the European business school landscape. A remarkable exception to this focus on US schools has been offered by Amdam et al. (2003), the authors having explicitly researched that which is promised by the book's subtitle, *The Content of European Business Education*, and having come up with some very strong arguments that there is indeed something like a genuinely European approach to management education, arguments which paved the way for much of our own research framework. Therefore, we decided to complement the Carnegie report of 2011 by presenting a report on European business schools (including, for reasons to be explained later, one Asian school), with the goal of investigating emerging practices of integrating the humanities and social sciences into transformative management education as well as the reasons for this integration, ideally offering some new ideas on such endeavours.

Consulting the Map: Historical and Research Notes

To investigate what factors might offer leverage for 'reinventing' management education (Steyaert et al., 2016) and what role the humanities and social sciences might play in this development, we think it appropriate to place our research object within its broader historical context, as if checking the location of our study on the map that we have used for its orientation, before introducing our research project itself.

Like other areas of professional education, such as, for instance, engineering, management education was brought into the fold of the university system relatively late. While what usually is referred to as the archetype of the European university had been established in 1809, with Wilhelm von Humboldt's founding of the first modern state university in Berlin, institutions which offered management education only began to "emerge during the Second Industrial Revolution (1880–1920)" and then not at first as part of universities but as separate institutions which "developed a strong focus on functional disciplines, reflecting a practical approach", most notably in the shape of the German *Handelshochschulen* and the French *Grandes écoles de commerce* (Amdam et al., 2003, p. 13). Some such schools (like the University of St. Gallen, which was originally founded as a *Handelshochschule*) evolved over the years into business universities, still retaining their specialisation but adopting the institutional structures and academic duties and privileges of full universities. Others became universities of applied science, keeping to a distinctly practical approach as opposed to the more research-oriented focus of universities. A third type of business schools emerged in the form of schools either incorporated into full universities (like, for example, ESADE at Barcelona, which was founded as an autonomous institution but today is part of Ramon Llull University) or set up within universities as part of their portfolio of schools.

The sheer diversity of these developmental histories helps to explain why, following Amdam et al. (2003), we decided to go for European business schools in our study. In some respects, the historical European academic tradition has impacted and still impacts differently on them compared to the development of Anglo-American business schools. Paradoxically, the main difference lies in the heterogeneity of institutional settings from which European business schools are working, since those settings often vary hugely due to the differences between the individual political systems in which they operate, differences which of course feedback into the respective institutions. In consequence, as Amdam et al. point out, "[r]ather than speaking about one European system of business education, it is more appropriate to speak about several nation specific systems of business education" (2003, p. 13), as opposed to the more streamlined systems framing Anglo-American (and especially US) business schools. As will be seen from the material we present in the following chapters, it is especially the role the humanities and social sciences play in transformative management education that, in all the schools we visited, is most closely linked to the cultural and political embeddedness of the respective institutions, thus mirroring the historically developed diversity of those systems. This means that, in terms of implementing and standardising the integration of the humanities and social sciences across their European diversity, let alone working towards the possibility of any kind of global standardisation, these schools face an added complexity which does not, as far as we can see, apply to Anglo-American business schools in equal measure.

There are, however, two more factors which influence the role of the humanities and social sciences here and which, while they may be slightly more pronounced in European business schools, are certainly more generally significant. The first of these factors is the rising tension between two different educational philosophies struggling for supremacy in academic management education. The roots of one of these philosophies go back to the ideological background of the Humboldtian university's founding. Humboldt had designed his institutional model to provide what he and his contemporaries in the aftermath of the Enlightenment movement called *Bildung*, that is, an education which was at least as much concerned with character-building and fostering abilities for curiosity-driven research as with the distribution of practically applicable skills (Thomä, 2005). Historically speaking, Humboldt's concept of *Bildung* is the precursor of Mezirow's concept of transformative education, and the latter, especially in the significance ascribed to rationality in his approach (Mezirow, 2009), works in many ways on almost identical lines of thought.

When business schools became part of the university landscape, this concept of *Bildung* had already lost much of its power, and the specific nature of management education eroded it further. Due to the content they researched and taught, business schools from the start maintained close ties to contemporary stakeholders in business and industry, not least because their faculty offered and still offer consulting and other services outside their respective schools as well as executive education. Since business schools were therefore much closer to the non-academic practitioner of management than to most of the other academic disciplines, and since they had to cater to the needs of non-academic practitioners as well as to those of their own students, who in turn expected mainly to be trained for the profession instead of for academic careers, these schools were and still are understood to offer a set of practically applicable skills, rather than Humboldt's holistic *Bildung*, in the manner of what we have often heard described as 'tool-boxes', ready to use as soon as graduates hit the job market.

One of the most prominent contemporary voices arguing for this instrumental approach towards management education is that of Howard Thomas and his co-authors, who have delivered several reports on management education over recent years. Thomas et al. are convinced that current academic management education fails to prepare students for "the market-place" (2014, p. 125) by failing to train them sufficiently in skills of practical applicability. The argument that Thomas et al. are presenting is not against integrated management education as such, far from it, as they firmly advocate increasing the input of the humanities and social sciences in the areas of business ethics, intercultural competence and critical thinking. Their argument is, however, very much in favour of providing students with added instrumental skills, including those that can be culled from the humanities and social sciences, instead of having them trained in exploratory academic research which not only is of no use to them practically but, even worse, effectively alienates them from the success-oriented mind-set that is perceived as necessary for dealing with the demands of their later jobs.

The other side of this debate is represented by voices like those of Gordon and Howell, who stated incisively that "[i]t *should be the primary object of collegiate business education to prepare students for personally fruitful and socially useful careers in business and related types of activity*" (1959, p. 47). Along similar lines, for the authors of the Carnegie report, the goal of education in general is to mould students into responsible citizens, enhancing "moral and civic understanding" by imparting "the capacity to interpret, judge, acquire knowledge of, and understand complex issues and institutions, and a sophisticated grasp of ethical and democratic principles", as well as "the motivation to do the right thing", which includes guiding "the individual's goals and values, interests, commitments, and convictions" and the "capacity for effective communication, including moral and political discourse; skills in political participation, the capacity to work effectively with people, including those who are very different from oneself; and the ability to organize other people for action" (Colby et al., 2003, pp. 99–100). According to Khurana (2007), management schools have failed signally in this, as the instrumental approach to management education reduces future managers, initially supposed to be societally responsible visionaries, to mere craftsmen hiring themselves out for the best possible salary. To remedy this, the authors of the Carnegie report of 2011 suggest, the focus on the instrumental needs to be replaced by a transformative philosophy of education, especially since, as they argue emphatically, students are being transformed by their studies anyway, so that it becomes imperative to make use of this process for guiding them instead of merely letting it happen accidentally:

> GOING TO COLLEGE CHANGES PEOPLE. Regardless of their age or stage in life, people's understanding of the world, themselves, and their sense of what is possible are affected by the experience of higher education [. . .]. In these ways, higher education is a deeply *formative* experience for all those who undergo it.
>
> *(Colby et al., 2011, p. 32; see also Pascarella & Terenzini, 2005)*

While the gap between these two educational philosophies has shaped the discourse on academic management education for a long time now, this gap has become even more marked over recent decades, mainly due to the pressure exerted on management education programmes around the world by the need for institutional accreditation which sprang up in the aftermath and as a direct consequence of the Bologna reform. The Humboldtian paradigm of *Bildung*, and now the concept of transformative education leaves and even demands much space for exploring and realising individual potential on the part of both students and teachers, making it, however, hard to evaluate precisely the learning outcomes achieved by the students, at least with the tools commonly used in institutional evaluations at present. Accreditations and rankings, on the other hand, work on the principle that such outcomes must be measurable to assure international comparability, having in consequence contributed to shape management education based on a logic that is fundamentally different from the idea of *Bildung*, instead following what has recently been described as an "alignment model": "The underlying assumption of this logic is the accessibility of every outcome in education, based on a more instrumental approach to learning and teaching" (Eberle & Metelmann, 2016, p. 410).

The development of this approach in academic management education has been facilitated by the second of the two factors mentioned earlier, namely the increasing disciplinary segregation of knowledge which also came with the Humboldtian university (Östling, 2018). This segregation was useful and even necessary at the time, built on a long-lasting process of emergence that would provide a manageable institutional framework for academic research and teaching. Over the decades before the University of Berlin was founded, it had become clear that emulating the *uomo universale* of the Renaissance era who was able at least to aim at knowing everything about anything, imagining the world as a stable entity where all knowledge was connected and thus could be thought and known as a whole, was no longer an attainable goal. The more differentiated the methods and instruments of research became, yielding increasingly complex masses of data to be processed, the more an organisational scheme was required to allow for both a reasonable division of labour and sustainable governing procedures, to which the structuring of the university according to disciplinary boundaries was the obvious answer.

The practical merits of this structuring, moreover, were based on a concept of knowledge which ideally, however, many disciplines were brought into the academic fold and held them together by the common factor of the similar rationality of their respective approaches. Until the second half of the eighteenth century, nature and, by extension, culture had been perceived as the mysterious agents of God's unfathomable powers of creation and thus as resources to which humans had limited access at most. The Enlightenment movement claimed the ability to think rationally for mankind as a means to overcome such limitations, at the same time secularising morality, which had been the sole domain of Christian faith, by declaring rational thought to be intrinsically moral, since its main goal at the time was considered to be that it should contribute actively to the common societal good. Academic research was perceived as realising such contributions by digging up as much knowledge as possible to add to the stock at the disposal of modern society's developmental dynamics. The notion of knowledge informing the modern academic landscape accordingly rested on the conviction that knowledge was basically there *a priori*, to be coaxed from the hidden places where it had lain dormant but had unquestionably existed all along as an entity whose only instability factor was the extent of the information to be found, while its respective characteristics were supposed to be clearly and unalterably set by reality itself. In other words, knowledge was understood as an ontologically given substance, with disciplinary variations at first mainly occurring through the choice of the object for research, while the processes of its recovery and interpretation were supposed to be virtually identical in all and any academic research and teaching.

In this context, at the time of the founding of the Humboldtian university, the humanities—whereas the social sciences, like management, became part of academic education only much later—played a major role, as they were supposed to be more or less the owners of rational thought. The German term *Geisteswissenschaften* that Humboldt introduced when installing them at the core of the European university defined dealing with *Geist* as the sole privilege of what then consisted mostly of the disciplines of philology, history and philosophy. *Geist*, which only vaguely translates as 'mind' or 'intellect', encodes the emancipatory potential of rational thought as the main moral and intellectual driving force of mankind's development since the Enlightenment had declared the autonomy of human thought; this, of course, was the reason for the term *Geisteswissenschaften* having been translated into English as 'humanities'. On the strength of this privilege, the humanities in Humboldt's university effectively inherited the role that the *artes liberales* had played in pre-modern university education. For more than 600 years before this, students entering academic education had had to go through a mandatory *studium generale* in the said *artes liberales* before they were allowed to move on to specialise in law, medicine or theology. Since the teaching of the latter three was designed to provide for standardised procedures and techniques, allowing for the ever-expanding states of the middle ages and early modernity to be governed and administered cohesively, the *artes liberales* were understood to guarantee similar frameworks of perception and values for any student who was to be employed by the state after graduation. Therefore, when Humboldt implemented his reform by placing the study of humanity in the Enlightenment sense of the word at its core, he centred it on the disciplines providing this tissue, defining their methodology as the most important benchmark for any scientific research and teaching.

Initially, this move was supposed to guarantee an academic corporate identity which ensured the harmonious coexistence of all and any disciplines gathered under the university's roof. In the long run, this design, however, proved too fragile to withstand the impact of the energies generated by the disciplinary specialisation which the design had allowed and even invited to emerge. As European universities reacted to the ever-increasing amount of knowledge to be classified and processed by adding more and more disciplines and sub-disciplines to their portfolio, the ontological understanding of knowledge which had informed the organisational segregation of disciplines fostered the equally ontological understanding that, if there were naturally given corpora of knowledge to be retrieved by specialised research, then of course the institutional entities who dealt with such research, i.e. the disciplines, were representing such corpora, secure in the conviction that the latter belonged to the former and vice versa. Inevitably, this led to academic disciplines drifting apart in far more than just their choice of topic and developing their own derivatives of rational thought which, towards the end of the nineteenth century, were barely recognisable as having come from the common notion of rationality that had once been supposed to constitute the university's corporate identity.

The first visible crack in the harmonious surface appeared when Wilhelm Dilthey in 1883 publicly declared that that the concept of knowledge represented by the humanities and social sciences was incompatible with that represented by the natural sciences, since the humanities were about understanding (*verstehen*) and the natural sciences about explaining (*erklären*) (Dilthey, 1989), leading to a vociferous debate between academics about which of the two types was more valuable to society. Neither of the parties bothered about even understanding, much less explaining to the non-academic public, that producing different types of knowledge, however incompatible, might be an achievement in itself which in fact could add to public value creation. The long-term consequences of this debate impacted badly on the public perception of academic teaching and research. When Charles Percy Snow in his Rede Lecture, *The Two Cultures*, in 1959, accused both humanities and natural science scholars of being too pre-occupied with their own concerns to pull their weight in meeting the global challenges of, among others, hunger and war in Third World countries (Snow, 1959), this mirrored the then widespread public opinion that universities, far from taking up the responsibility for public welfare that Humboldt had defined as the university's ultimate mission, had allowed their scholars to become so wrapped up in their own esoteric concerns that they had effectively divorced themselves from reality.

For the humanities this development proved disastrous, as they had never bothered to develop a branding narrative to explain their value for society to the broader public, having complacently felt so sure of their inherited academic status that they had not paid much attention to what was happening around them; thus the humanities abruptly found themselves in a situation where more and more universities began to cut down on their funding, on the strength of Snow's and other arguments. It was the social sciences and, more specifically, sociology— which had become an academic discipline at roughly the same time as management studies—that in the 1970s came up with a concept which today may well be crucial in leading the way towards the humanities' and social sciences' successful integration into transformative management education. Taking Dilthey's argument to a new level, the Sociology of Scientific Knowledge (SSK), which quickly established itself as an influential sub-discipline of sociology in its own right, "insisted that science was interestingly and constitutively social all the way to its technical core: scientific knowledge itself had to be understood as a social product" (Pickering, 1992, p. 1). SSK saw "the technical culture of science as a single conceptual framework" (1992, p. 4), basically arguing that this 'technical culture', i.e. both the methodology of research and its practice, shapes the outcome of research according to the researching actors' interests. Most importantly, the term 'interest' in this context does not (or at least not only) apply to the open-minded scientific curiosity for unknown facts that is usually—idealistically—associated with scientific research, but rather to the individual or collective agenda of the respective agents involved:

> On the one hand, actors can be seen as tentatively seeking to extend culture in ways that might serve their interests rather than in ways it might not. And on the other hand, interests serve as standards against which the products of such extensions, new conceptual nets, can be assessed.
>
> *(1992, p. 4)*

In consequence, "scientific knowledge has to be seen, not as the transparent representation of nature", as the ontological notion of knowledge has it, "but rather as a knowledge relative to a particular culture" (1992, p. 5), which is at least partly produced to satisfy this culture's needs and to provide for its long-term stability—a concept which laid the foundation for much of Mezirow's approach to transformative learning through the epistemological reappraisal of the frameworks of value that students take ontologically for granted when they enter university.

Though the SSK draws its conclusions mainly from empirical research into the research practices of the natural sciences, it takes no great leap of imagination to realise how those conclusions also apply to the production of knowledge performed by academic business schools, especially as the impact of interest on research agents' practice seems at least as evident here as it is in the natural sciences. Academic business schools' research today certainly is a 'social product', in Pickering's phrase (1992), since a "substantial amount of new management knowledge, defined as management concepts, has emerged outside academic institutions over the last twenty years" (Amdam et al., 2003, p. 21), which is then fed back into and thus influences academic research through the close ties that most management education faculty build up with the business environment outside universities (cf. also the VUCA-paradigm). This means that management research produces a certain type of knowledge shaped both by research methodology and interest, both factors usually more or less dependent on each other, the product itself thus being far more of a cultural construction than a collection of given facts. Though this notion has in fact been around for quite a long time, as John Dewey already put it forward in 1929 in *The Quest for Certainty: A Study of the Relation of Knowledge and Action* (Dewey, 1984), it is only now beginning to be taken up by management education research (see e.g. Statler & Salovaara, 2016).

There are several observations to be noted in the light of our historical mapping which have a notable impact on the integration of the humanities and social sciences into transformative management education today. For one thing, the history of the European university shows that the idea of transformative education, far from being invented by Mezirow and his peers, was in fact already a part—and even the declared mission—of the modern university's initial set up. Furthermore, the humanities and later the social sciences were for a fairly long time perceived as its main actors, which may explain why many business schools are turning towards them today, associating them mainly with ethical and moral issues in a kind of collective memory of the humanities once having represented rational as moral thinking.

For another thing, the tension between instrumental and transformative educational philosophies seems to be tied to the historical rupture between types of disciplines and, in consequence, types of knowledge instilled by Dilthey's critique of the Enlightenment's normative understanding of rationality. It was precisely at the time when the debates engendered by this rupture went viral that management education became part of the university landscape, which means that Humboldt's concept of *Bildung*, with its underlying ontological notion of knowledge, had already lost much of its influence on academia and, especially in management education, was about to lose even more of this influence, since the object of management research from the start demanded a certain amount of epistemo-logical awareness which had not been part of the Humboldtian university's initial make-up.

Lastly, it needs to be underscored that the Humboldtian university was not originally designed as the ivory tower, sheltering scholars from reality, which it became during the nineteenth century. Rather, it was founded as an institution to contribute to society as a whole by providing research and education which, by virtue of being conducted rationally, were moral in the sense that they pro-moted the common good. Thus, the current debate on management education, especially in the light of the recent financial crises, might be perceived as bringing academic education back to its early nineteenth-century roots, investigating ways and means to increase its added value to society—or at least its recognition by the public—on terms which link transformative education, performed with the help of the humanities and social sciences, to re-establishing and/or making vis-ible their commitment to frameworks of value which closely resemble those that Humboldt and his peers believed to be indispensable for the university's ability to contribute to the common good.

On the Way: The "Humanities' Business" Project's Research Design

As has already been evidenced by our choice of title for our report, we chose transformation theory as shaped by Mezirow and others as the mainstay of our theoretical framework. Based on this, the general leading question for our research project aimed at finding out how the integration of the humanities and social sciences into management education contributes to shifting the latter from an instrumental to a more transformative approach to teaching and learning. This question, of course, frames what is known as a 'wicked problem', that is, a problem which has no clear-cut solution and may even possibly have none at all, or at least not a generalisable one, since, for a start, business schools tend to differ hugely depending on their governance structures, individual histories and respective cul-tural contexts. Furthermore, the concepts blithely put forward in this question are by no means covered by a common consensus about what precisely they mean, beginning with the concept of integration itself, going on to who and what exactly the humanities and social sciences are and, last but not least, to what con-cepts of management inform business schools' educational philosophies.

Therefore, we decided from the start to conduct a field study with a sample group of eight to ten business schools by performing semi-structured interviews over several days which would be taped, transcribed and then analysed quanti-tatively and qualitatively. The method applied to this analysis is a hybrid derived from the fact that, on the one hand, all members of the team brought significant previous experience in harvesting and analysing empirical data to the project; Jörg Metelmann, for example, worked as project partner for McKinsey and manager of a start-up in coaching and consultancy before he decided to re-enter academia. On the other hand, we knew from the start that our disciplinary professional training would colour both our findings and their analysis: Ulrike Landfester and Jörg Metelmann are both philologists by training, while Nicolaj Tofte Brenneche received a philosophical as well as a management education at Copenhagen Business School (CBS), and Queralt Prat-i-Pubill, having studied at ESADE where the humanities and social sciences are part of the curricula, had a similar background. Therefore, we planned to put this training to analytical use, going for a narratological approach: we would look for similarities and differences in the ways in which our interviewees talked about the humanities and social sciences in management education, in the choices of topics and in the manner in which those topics were being made sense of—looking, in short, for narrative patterns in the respective institutions' discursive processing of their experiences and opinions. The results would then be linked to the available facts about the institutions that we were going to select.

The selection of our case studies was informed by three parameters. One was that we wanted to conduct a study focusing on Europe—not, it must be emphasised, out of some mistaken notion that Europe does everything (or even anything) better than the rest of the world, but because we wanted to complement the existing reports, as mentioned earlier. However, to balance this Eurocentrism, we decided that we would include at least one non-European business school, as well as selecting at least one business school definitely not including the humanities and social sciences in their curricula (as long as they were prepared to talk to us about this, of course). The second parameter was that we would focus on institutions offering mainly undergraduate education, so as to keep the cases comparable, as postgraduate education quite often works on the basis of different logics, both institutionally and in its content. The third parameter was the comparability of our sample group in terms of international reputation, which meant that we planned our initial survey to include all European business and management schools accredited by the Association to Advance Collegiate Schools of Business (AACSB) (86 in total in 2014). Additionally, we included the business schools which were, like HSG, part of the CEMS Global Alliance in Management Education network—the network's name once read "Community of European Management Schools", hence the acronym—as the CEMS master's in international management is both consistently highly ranked and features a strong component of humanities and social science contributions in its curriculum (21 non-AACSB-accredited CEMS partners), which means that we contacted a total population of 107 institutions, regardless of whether they were officially working with the humanities and social sciences or not, as at this stage we wanted to remain open for any unofficial and/or emergent activities as well.

To develop the catalogue of questions both for the first survey and later on for our interviews, we used the strategic triangle that Benington and Moore proposed in 2011 as a guideline for the creation of public value—that is, define public value, ensure authorisation and mobilise operational implementation (Bening-ton & Moore, 2011, p. 4)—as a starting point. Proceeding from this, we formulated three questions for the first survey which were designed as far as possible to avoid offering implicit answers:

1. Does your institution practise on any level the integration of the humanities and social sciences into management education (course, programme, department, university level, etc.)?
2. If so, at what stage of education are the students confronted with elements from the humanities and social sciences (undergraduate, postgraduate, post-doctoral, executive education)?
3. Is the integration of the humanities and social sciences into management education at your institution an issue of strategic import on any level and at any stage of emergence (e.g. only just beginning to be discussed informally or firmly established in the institution's mission statement)?

This questionnaire was sent from the HSG president's office to the deans and/or presidents of the respective institutions. It was redistributed as a reminder twice and was responded to by 22 institutions, of which 20 answered affirmatively. Eight of the latter, though signalling interest in the topic as such, indicated that they were not practising the integration of the humanities and social sciences on any level.

For the remaining 12 institutions, we performed case assessments by evaluating the responses given in the answering mails together with the material available on the institutions' websites. The team then discussed the preliminary results, to prepare phone and/or Skype interviews with the persons who had responded, so that those interviews would yield approximately the same type and level of information. The main points of interest then were the implicit or explicit endorsement of integrating the humanities and social sciences into management education by the respective school's governance, the impact on undergraduate curricula and the mechanisms that were in place to implement and stabilise this integration and evaluate its results.

Based on those assessments, we selected eight institutions for site visits, namely

Copenhagen Business School (CBS)
ESADE, Barcelona (ESADE)
Koç University, Istanbul (Koç)
Lancaster University Management School (LUMS)
Stockholm School of Economics (SSE)
University of St. Gallen (HSG)
Aalto University School of Business (Aalto)
Singapore Management University (SMU)

The final selection of these institutions reflects several concerns, first among them being our goal to document as many different approaches to integrating the humanities and social sciences into management education as possible. That means that the institutions we did not select in the second screening round were certainly as interesting and dynamic as the others, but that in the end we went for maximum variety in terms of degrees of developmental maturity of integrative education and diversity of lead motives for establishing it, as opposed to highlighting similarities. Two of the institutions we selected, however (SMU and Aalto), need further explanation. We choose SMU because it was the one institution among the business schools we contacted which has recently engaged in strengthening the contribution of the humanities and social sciences to management education through a strategic decision by the president and the university governing board, resulting in a reform process conducted top-down which promised—and later yielded—extremely interesting insights into the manifold challenges posed by such a decision. Aalto, on the other hand, we chose due to the fact that, even though they responded positively to our initial survey, we were told in no uncertain terms that they had not even considered the integration of the humanities and social sciences when recently merging a business school, a technical university and a school of arts and design into what today is Aalto University—even though the contribution of the latter school is seen as crucial to the spirit of interdisciplinary teaching and research at the core of the newly created university. Thus, both SMU and Aalto were selected as touchstones for the discourse on integrated management education that we found at the institutions we screened.

Based on the case assessments, we developed eight pre-visit case reports which were shared with and commented on by the contact persons at the respective institutions before the site visits. The purpose of the pre-visit reports was to ensure accuracy in our description of the various institutions as far as possible, as well as to provide the overall context for our questions both to us and to the interviewees. At this stage, we retained the framework of our initial questionnaire but adapted the guidelines for our interviews to the respective institutional settings so as to develop a comprehensive picture of their practices. Basically, in line with the strategic triangle mentioned earlier, in all the interviews, we focused on the following set of questions. How did our interviewees define the contribution of the humanities and social sciences to integrated management education, in terms of both added value for management education and of its public value as a whole? How and by whom was such integration authorised? What stage of implementation had been reached in the organisation, in what manner and what was the ultimate goal?

Between autumn 2014 and spring 2015, we conducted our site visits in teams of two, assigning different pairings to each of these visits so as to avoid bias on our side due to the forming of interactional habits. Each site visit lasted between two and three days. During the visits we interviewed students, teaching faculty, programme directors, deans and, if available, presidents as well as members of the respective schools' governing boards and councils; we also visited classes pointed out to us by the institutions as being representative for what they aspired to accomplish under the heading of integrating the humanities and social sciences into management education. A full list of our interviewees is given in the Appendix, together with a panorama of the cases. Most interviews were done with individuals, but a few were also conducted as group interviews. After the site visits, the taped interviews were fully transcribed by the researchers who had conducted the visits and distributed to the whole team, together with the sound files of the recordings. This way, the material resulting from each of the site visits, together with any further documentation the respective institutions provided afterwards, was reviewed by the whole team before being subsequently aligned in terms of case protocols comprising a general introduction to each institution and the transcripts of the interviews.

There are, of course, some limitations to our study. We know, for instance, that several schools we contacted with our first survey and who responded either in the negative or not at all, are in fact practising the integration of the humanities and social sciences, but as our resources were limited, we could not afford to go after them more proactively beyond redistributing our survey. Also, though we do stand by our aim to create a European 'Carnegie report', we are aware that, having restricted ourselves mainly to European business schools, the potentially valuable contributions of non-European schools have been left out. Last, but not least, due to the 'wicked' nature of the problem that we were researching, our questions were rather explorative in character and the answers correspondingly yielded highly diverse narratives both in style and content so that our analytical categories needed some leeway in order to accommodate our material—which might, strictly speaking, be considered as taking unwarranted liberties with it, of which we discuss more next.

Nearly There: Deciding on Narrative Strategies for the Report

As we have just pointed out, the analysis of our material on the 'wicked problem' of how to create public value by integrating the humanities and social sciences into transformative management education proved a challenge in terms of applying comparable categories. Consequently, shaping both the material and its analysis into a report worthy of the name necessitated some major methodological reflections on our mode of presentation. So we first looked for orientation to other reports on management education and found that such reports are usually characterised by one of three types of narrative which can, of course, be combined with each other but more often are employed fairly pure: the genealogical narrative, which explains management education historically; the diagnostic narrative, which presents itself as a mere collation of facts; and the programmatic narrative, which from the beginning shows itself to have a clearly defined agenda and composes the material it uses accordingly (Landfester et al., 2016).

All of these narratives, we found, even the diagnostic narrative, use techniques of discursive presentation which to varying extents take the liberties to which we have admitted earlier. Since Hayden White published his book *The Content of the Form: Narrative Discourse and Historical Representation* in 1987, it has become common knowledge that such liberties cannot be avoided by any type of discursive presentation, since, however ontologically sound the findings of empirical research may be, shaping them into a coherent text cannot but influence the content of what has been researched, starting with the selection of quotations—which leaves others out—and the grouping of the findings into clusters which may or may not represent reality, but in any case are representing the author's or authors' choices at least as much (White, 1987). In our case, those choices are already reflected in the exploratory nature of our interviews' form and content, so that we had to find a narrative framework at least to make those choices as transparent and visible as possible.

On the strength of these deliberations, we took two basic decisions. One was to keep true to both the explorative spirit in which we conducted our interviews and the importance which we placed from the start on similarities in narrative patterns and on the choice of topics that our interviewees emphasised through them. This means that we decided to align the structure of our chapters according to the recurrence of such patterns and topic choices rather than, for instance, dedicating chapters to each school in turn. Technically, this would, of course, have been possible, but it would not have squared well with our goal to find common ground and perhaps even a common discourse on integrating the humanities and social sciences into transformative management education in our sample group, which then might lead us to some generalisable conclusions. As we know that the resulting compilation of different voices from different schools under the same chapter headings may seem disorientating to the reader, we have included a panorama of cases in our Appendix, placing those voices in their respective institutional contexts.

The second decision we took was to use all three narrative modes outlined earlier in combination, assigning those modes explicitly to the respective parts of our text. Thus, we offer our Introduction in the mode of a genealogical narrative on both the object of our research and the history of our project. The presentation of the material that we harvested in our interviews, in the following three core chapters of our report, we kept mostly in the diagnostic mode, letting as many of our interviewees as we dared—considering the overwhelming richness of the material—speak for themselves. Each chapter, however, finishes with a programmatic part which offers our conclusions and the practical suggestions that we developed from our findings. The last chapter focuses on the question whether and, if so, how the integration of the humanities and social sciences can add to the public value of business schools; the chapter is designed to be purely programmatic, putting forth our ideas on what this public value could or should be and how the humanities could and should contribute to it—ideas which have been inspired by our material but are not necessarily covered by its content to their full extent, so we feel particularly obliged to take responsibility for this last part.

The Point(s) of Arrival: Key Findings and Chapter Structure

We found that there were three main areas of interest concerning the integration of the humanities and social sciences into management education which were consistently brought up at all of the business schools we visited: firstly, the educational philosophy or philosophies informing such integrational endeavours, that is, the question of what exactly transformative management education needs or wants to achieve; secondly, the issue of interdisciplinary education and its practices and learning goals; and, finally, the challenges of strategically positioning integrated management education both internally and in the political and societal contexts embedding the respective schools. Accordingly, we present our material in three chapters to reflect this clustering of findings.

The material presented in our second chapter, "Transforming Education: Philosophies and Practices", is mainly concerned with the perspectives of students and teachers on the role of the humanities and social sciences in transformative management education, since students and teachers are obviously the stakeholder groups most directly confronted with the consequences of management education turning transformative with the help of the humanities and social sciences. Our key finding here is that both teachers and students engaging with this type of education often struggle with a deep-seated habit of perceiving management education as following an instrumental rather than a transformative approach, along with the fact that, in addition to this mind-set, the organisational structures of contemporary universities do not easily lend themselves to transformative education.

This finding is closely linked to the material we present in our third chapter, "Transforming Knowledge: Towards Tomorrow's Needs". Both the instrumental perception of management education and the university's organisational structures seem to rest on the ontological concept of knowledge shaped by the system of disciplinary segregation. The project of integrating the humanities and social sciences into management education with a view to rendering the latter more transformative therefore regularly runs up against the notion that, however much interdisciplinary teaching and research is recognised as necessary to the future of management education and however much hope is placed in the humanities and social sciences playing an important part in this, disciplinary boundaries are still closely protected—or at least not willingly breached actively by all sides concerned. That this should be so is mostly not, it has to be said, the result of active resistance, but a mixture of the lack of any canonised knowledge about how precisely to go about it and of a set of clichés about other disciplines which are obviously very hard to shake.

This un- or semi-conscious resistance is in turn linked to the key finding of our fourth chapter, "Transforming Business Schools: Strategic Challenges". Since the organisational structures of universities are not usually very congenial to transformative teaching practices, the latter will demand a lot of extra effort, especially on the part of teachers and programme managers, to implement them sustainably. This is due to two factors, namely to the academic privileges of teaching and research, on the one hand, which make it difficult to lead unwilling colleagues towards cooperating with endeavours likely to take them out of their comfort zones. On the other hand, even business schools which actively engage in transformative management education by integrating non-canonical disciplines like the humanities and social sciences often find it equally difficult to square such endeavours with the demands of global standardisation.

All three chapters are structured similarly in that, in their first part, they present our findings in the diagnostic mode, which means that we take up the main threads of topics turning up repeatedly so as to group our material accordingly, leaving our interviewees' input to speak for itself, however, without interpreting it any more than by its selection and configuration. Our own interpretation, that is, our conclusions and suggestions derived from this input, is given in the second part of these chapters in the programmatic mode, offering observations and ideas as to where, in our eyes, the roots of the problems brought up by our interviewees might be looked for—and what might possibly be done about solving them.

Our fifth and final chapter, "A Business Schools' Guide to the Galaxy of Transformative Management Education", presents a short summary of those programmatic narratives, linking our conclusions and suggestions about the question of what public value business schools do, can or should produce—without, as needs to be said at the outset, even trying to set up a normative frame of reference for this, since we are convinced that transformative management education conducted with the help of the humanities and social sciences should be about the process of reflecting on agendas instead of just imperatively setting them. However, both the programmatic parts of Chapters 2–4 and our final chapter include quite a number of critical observations on current practices and their historical and institutional background, as well as some rather pointed statements about educational politics which might be considered deliberately provoking—which is true only in so far as we firmly believe that presenting our research is not about claiming to have exhausted our topic in any way but, on the contrary, about engaging in further discussions, to which we very much look forward.

2

TRANSFORMING EDUCATION

Philosophies and Practices

The main title we chose for this chapter—like those we chose for the following two—is intentionally ambiguous, reflecting a phenomenon we found at all the business schools we visited: while our interviewees were very much aware that going for transformative education by integrating the humanities and social sciences naturally meant, in the first place, enabling students to go through education as a transformative process, this goal also meant transforming the concept of academic transformation itself. The statements we present next clearly show this ambiguity, since they were made more often than not in view of an institutional context which, while committing to transformative education in various degrees of determination, still did not easily accommodate its implementation and thus needed to be taken into account when calibrating its potential for success.

The questions we put to our interviewees in this area focused mainly on two issues. One was their personal experience with management education including the humanities and social sciences, asking what teaching techniques they used to bridge the gaps between 'classical' content and methodology, and the content and methodology provided by the humanities and social sciences. The other issue concerned their views on the educational philosophy behind this type of teaching and learning, asking whether including the humanities and social sciences made a difference to their didactic frame of reference and, if so, what role they expected or perceived these disciplines to play in it.

The answers we received addressed four topics, according to which we structured this chapter. First, the perspective of students on management education, taking account of their needs and expectations, is of growing importance both to teachers and students themselves, indicating that transformative management education means focusing more on the students than on the subjects taught. Second, discussing transformative teaching of course begged the question or rather questions as to how teachers are supposed to go about it practically, especially in the area of defining learning goals and assessing whether they have been reached or not. Third, the part that the humanities and social sciences could or should play in transformative education, interestingly, was most often brought up in relation to the practical applicability of its content, based both on the concept of practice projected by academic management education as such, on the one hand, and the expectation and/or experience that the transformational element contributed by the humanities and social sciences was an enhancement of practical rather than theoretical knowledge, on the other; it is therefore mainly in this part of the chapter that the assumptions about the functional relation between the humanities' and social sciences' contribution to management education and the shift towards transformative learning and teaching are discussed. Fourth, we present several courses designed to include material from the humanities and social sciences from different schools, to illustrate the statements collected in the third part of the chapter through examples of teaching practice.

"The Primary Focus Is Not the Subject, but the Student": Instrumental Versus Transformative Education

"We need to create an approach in which the primary focus is not the subject, but the student", Josep Lozano, professor of business ethics and corporate social responsibility at ESADE's Department of Social sciences, told us decisively. In his eyes, management education has, by concentrating on imparting skills, lost sight of its most important stakeholders, i.e. the students:

> We don't start with the students' experiences, but always with future situations. We need to be focused on the reality on the students, help them to reflect upon their current experiences, about corruption in their daily lives or in their free time—how do they behave in the cafeteria, for example. [. . .] We sell them that we offer information and [will] be with you at the start of your career, but we don't tell them that they are in a process of lifelong learning; we have to transmit the idea that to be a good manager is not only about attending the classes.
>
> *(interview, 2015)*

In a similar vein, Omid Ashari, professor at the HSG School of Management and programme director of the highly ranked master's in strategy and international management, emphasised that, for students, life outside their course-work during their studies shaped them far more than the courses themselves:

> To me, the real thing that happens, happens between the lines, between the courses, in the unofficial arena of a programme, that is where the nontypical business qualities are happening. There is where the transformation, the

development takes place. It is part of our core work, though those qualities would not be easily admitted by management.

(interview, 2015)

Instrumental management education is presented to students as offering a canonised body of knowledge to be absorbed in a prescribed time-span, creating the illusion that after absorption, having been sealed with a degree, this body of knowledge would then serve them as a tool-box adequate to any professional challenge. Instead, Lozano argued, management schools should enter into what he called an "anthropological debate":

> What's the kind of profiles [that] we want to promote? From there we can tackle different perspectives. What is the ideal student in the end, if we do our job very well? This question is missing! [W]e cannot separate personal and professional quality any more, but we are still under the classical distinction.
>
> *(interview, 2015)*

This distinction between the personal and the professional aspects of education is seen to be an effect of the instrumental understanding of management education, as this understanding allows and even promotes the divorcing of students' personal development from the acquisition of skills which are perceived as being useful but ostensibly exerting no influence whatsoever on their intellectual and emotional frameworks. Projected outwards through the societal image of management schools, this division palpably shapes students' expectations of management education, in what might be called a vicious circle: perceived to be professionally effective precisely because of this distinction between the professional and the personal, management schools attract students who are thus predisposed to view their education as primarily instrumental from the start, often having been trained towards this attitude by previous educational experiences. Jesper Blomberg at SSE stated that, in his experience, on entering university

> students don't know what they want, what they need. They come to, one, get a career, two, get intellectually stimulated, but this is what they say. They are very good at presenting themselves as professionals even before they know anything.
>
> *(interview, 2015)*

The then-president of Koç University, Professor Ümran İnan, told us that

> [w]hen students arrive [at] Koç University they are excellent in exam-manship. This is the main characteristic of our incoming students. For the student who has been groomed for exam performance, the first philosophy course hits him like a train.
>
> *(interview, 2014)*

On a similar note, Annemette Kjærgaard from CBS felt that first-year students were often less than ready for what awaited them in their academic education:

> Also, we need academic socialisation, they are not prepared to enter [...] university. They have been very much supported, they are not independent, motivated intrinsically, they are not used to mobilise themselves in what they do.
>
> *(interview, 2014)*

Students, therefore, do not open up easily to learning experiences which take them out of their intellectual comfort zone, especially if and when those experiences are derived from or linked to disciplines whose average societal image, like that of the humanities and social sciences, does not *a priori* promise practical applicability. Cecile Rozuel, teaching fellow at the LUMS Department of Organisation, Work and Technology, explained that she found it hard to get students interested in reflective discussion of business ethics because they are reluctant to engage with her interdisciplinary approach to it:

> Management in the way that I feel it's defined in management and business schools tries so much to have an identity of its own, to define itself as a profession, that when you try to bring the students back to "Aren't you a human being to start with?", all the questions that you can address from philosophy, sociology, psychology, depending on what you prefer, they can't really handle that because it doesn't feel like it's valued at all.
>
> *(interview, 2015)*

Rozuel's statement points to a problem which was of major concern at most of the schools we visited. The habits of instrumental learning, together with the fact that tuition fees in some European countries are steadily rising, seem to encourage a point of view among students according to which, as Sven Bislev, vice-dean of the Department of Management, Politics and Philosophy at CBS, described it, the relationship between the school and the student is analogous to that between buyer and seller:

> There is a tendency to understand education as a service, therefore they are customers and our role is to deliver the right material to them, but we need to do better. The idea of them being involved in a developmental dialogue with professors takes time for them. Because they need to understand the idea that they are not only being served but also invited to a trajectory.
>
> *(interview, 2014)*

For Bislev, it is clear that the experience of management education should be transformative:

> In the travel to being a qualified graduate, students undergo personal development. Part of learning how to act is to develop yourself as a

person, to be able to disregard prejudices, disregard [your] own interests, disregard easy buzz-words and combine analytical insight with the limited time you have for action and the limited frame you have for action. This picture is very much in synch with the requirements of MBA and Executive education, but in our university programmes we do not speak about personal development. There is a reluctance to engage with students as persons, the Americans are much more blunt in this aspect, they are not afraid of telling students what is good and what is bad, we are reluctant. We should confront the issue, moving the students from the opportunist view they have of the school: "[The] school teaches me how to make money", "I read these books because I am told so to pass the exams". Move them to a more engaged approach where they develop notions about their own competences, and possibilities and preferences, and engage us in discussions about these. It is a mutual interaction among teachers and students.

(interview, 2014)

In countries with high tuition fees, however, to act on the conviction that learning should be transformative and to employ the humanities and social sciences towards this goal is more difficult than in countries with lower fees, as students with a high debt load due to those fees are proportionally more dependent on standardised employability ratings, which leads to the contribution of the humanities and social sciences coming under even more scrutiny in terms of their practical applicability. "The instrumental demand on humanities is related to this strong pressure generated by the debt of tuition fees", as Sue Cox, dean emerita at LUMS, put it. She added,

It's really unfair, inter-generationally seen. You've got to link what you are offering to a job-market employability context. You have to say, "These are the core competences that the employers are looking for". And thinking in different domains and working across borders is one such essential competence.

(interview, 2015)

To foster this competence within an academic framework oriented so strongly towards the employability of its graduates means mainly, as Bogdan Costea, at the LUMS Department of Organisation, Work and Technology, told us, to try to align the expectations of the students with those of their future employers. Costea, being active at many recruiting events of LUMS and thus regularly in contact with future employers, found that they are usually looking for employees with a generalist educational background, expecting them to be flexible, capable of critical thought and of integrated problem-solving, including making use of other disciplines' methodologies, while students themselves tended to view one-track specialisation as the most promising way in which to enter the labour market:

> Of course, this is hard: to recruit students and to integrate. Employability remains a central theme among prospective students, even though it is performativity, not technical skills, which are sought after in the job market.
>
> *(interview, 2015)*

Among the students we talked to, on the other hand, we found none who admitted to preferring instrumental to transformative learning, though we have to assume that this was an effect of self-selection among the sample we met, since, from our observations, only students who were already involved on some level with transformative learning took up our invitation for interviews. At SSE, for example, we met with Isak, majoring in banking and finance, who was also the director of the students' Art Initiative and who presented the initiative's activities as an effort to shake up the SSE community by exposing it to unexpected and even provocative artworks, insisting that it was the emotional experience of such exposure, as opposed to the intellectual mainstream of 'logical empiricism' which characterised the school's research and teaching, that inspired transformation most effectively: "First you have to gain experience, then you can open up—not the talking first" (interview, 2015).

That students like Isak and others we met might not be representative of the larger student population was also made clear to us when, at CBS, Maiken, Katrin and Helene, three students taking the course Business, Politics and Society in the BA programme business administration and society, one of the CBS programmes integrating humanities and social sciences content into management studies, told us (amid much laughter) that fellow students from the more traditional—they called it "hard-core"—BA programme international business explicitly took them for mere "pretenders" to management studies: "They tell us: 'You are so vague'!" All three of them saw nothing to worry about in this rather elitist attitude, as they saw themselves as the real elite:

> We think differently. We don't look only at profit and efficiency but we want to know how to motivate people to be efficient. We want to take people into the picture and also social concepts. We want to understand things, not just take them as given such as someone, say, from managerial economics. We want to be successful on a social basis.
>
> *(interview, 2014)*

To achieve this through the type of education offered by the BA in international business or the BA in sociology and management, students are led to engage systematically with interdisciplinary knowledge transfer. Sine Just, one of the directors of the programme Sociology and Management, explained that this was done practically by teaching different courses and then having students go through joint exams for those courses. A group of students from Just's programme told us about their experiences:

> There is a whole process of more and more integration throughout the programme, so we start by, one, understanding the basic concepts, two, understanding the context and complexities and, three, move towards processes. [. . .] We might not manage to make the integration in one course, but then we do the joint exams, [. . .] two courses in each field, and we had one exam; we were supposed to integrate what we learnt in five pages. Some things are easier to integrate. We had to integrate four courses in one exam. The problem is that after this experience we started wanting to link everything, always looking for the connections.
>
> *(interview, 2014)*

HSG, like CBS, has a long tradition in integrated management education. Unlike at CBS, however, where students can choose between integrated programmes and others, at HSG all students are obliged to participate in the Contextual Studies programme, meaning that each student is exposed to a certain amount of knowledge from the humanities and social sciences. For Dardan, student of business administration and then-president of the Student Union, this was one of the main reasons for coming to HSG:

> From friends I knew that in St. Gallen you could combine core subjects with contextual studies focusing more on this integrative management thinking—and I was attracted to the student culture with all the student clubs and opportunities—so, the educational structure and the student culture was important. [. . .] I actually asked some students yesterday why they chose to study here. There [are] always some students who mainly look at the name and reputation of HSG. But many also point to the educational approach.
>
> *(interview, 2015)*

When we asked whether and how this approach actually worked, Sarah, who was studying economics and was the Student Union's board member for student interests, told us,

> It depends a lot on the course and the teacher. I find it really cool if I can apply what I have learned previously in new courses—if the professor invites us to use what we learned in economics to study entirely different kinds of problems than we normally do in the economics programme, putting a sort of economics-spin on unusual problems, seen from an economics perspective. And then I find it really interesting to meet and work with students from other programmes and see how differently we approach problems.
>
> *(interview, 2015)*

As to the structure of the programme as a whole, Dardan and Sarah had different opinions, mirroring more or less the two main positions in the ongoing debate among HSG faculty about whether contextual studies should engage closer with the core subjects or whether they should stick to a broad diversity of subjects which would both allow and challenge the students to choose. Dardan, pointing out that contextual studies were about introducing students to the social, political and cultural contexts of their core subjects, firmly came down on the side of closer structural engagement—saying that "this would give you the opportunity to reflect; in the core you get the 'answers' on how markets work, but you need to reflect about this"—while Sarah argued in favour of diversity:

> I see the point of view but I don't know if I would like it. Obviously, it would add layers to your understanding of economics. I'm not sure I would like to be a person who only studied economics from different perspectives. We should have these discussions in the core programmes. In the contextual studies [we] should keep it open.
>
> *(interview, 2015)*

Both agreed that the transformational effects of contextual studies depended not only on the teachers but also very much on the mind-set of the students themselves. "It has a lot to do with the responsibility of the students. You have to want to learn in that way", Dardan said, and Sarah added,

> I focus on courses that I am really interested in. I know a lot of the teachers too so I know which ones have courses with a lot of discussion. [. . .] I think you have to make your own fun out of the contextual studies. If you have a passive attitude you won't get much out of it.
>
> *(interview, 2015)*

However, both also pointed out that in fact students tended to select contextual studies courses not so much for their subjects but rather with a view to how to get their credit points with the least effort: "The reality is often that students only choose courses they know they can do and get a good grade—not because they are interested in the course as such", Dardan told us. Sarah remarked, with a grin, that this technique was very much in keeping with the doctrine of profit maximisation taught in the HSG core courses—"This is what we learn, right?"—and she elaborated that, in fact, HSG during the first so-called Assessment Year itself pushed students towards this attitude by over-emphasising the instrumental at the cost of transformative learning:

> Of course, you learn in the Assessment Year to not understand everything— if you try, you are likely to fail—but to learn everything by heart and then pass. This is what you learn about learning at the Assessment Year.
>
> *(interview, 2015)*

The result of this initial learning experience was that, in later years, when the structured workload became less heavy and the choices more individual, the acquired habit of instrumental learning was hard to shake, as Ulrich Schmid, professor of Russian culture and society at the HSG School of Humanities and Social Sciences, and involved with the reform of the Contextual Studies programme, corroborated from his own teaching experience,

> students are very good in making presentations here. They learn this already during Assessment Year. In a way, they are also less creative here than elsewhere. Their approach is very streamlined. I try to hinder them to use their 'templates' by stressing [that they should] focus on problems rather than summarising 'facts' and 'chronological event bullet points', etc. All such dead [pieces of] information are two clicks away, so it is important to get them away from this autopilot engagement.
>
> *(interview, 2015)*

All in all, two major points stood out in the material we gathered on students' attitudes to integrated management education. The first of these points is that our interviewees saw traditional management education as focusing too much on imparting standardised skills and too little on the students' needs and expectations, the normative implication being that management education should be modelled on the former rather than on the latter in order to achieve its goals. The second point, closely linked to the first, is that students' needs and expectations are obviously far from being one and the same thing. Students' expectations of management education are shaped by factors such as the societal images of management studies and the humanities and social sciences, respectively, the habits of instrumental learning that have been ingrained both by previous learning experiences and the perceived nature of management education, and finally the pressure exerted by the perceived conditions of the labour market. These factors, however, seem to be operationalised by students habitually and opportunistically, rather than through conscious, critically reflected individual decisions, not least due to the fact that even schools which practise integrated and transformational management education at the same time systematically retain default settings like, for example, the Assessment Year at HSG, which incentivise precisely those instrumental learning techniques that transformational teaching is trying to overcome.

"So Basically I Teach Myself": Transformative Versus Instrumental Teaching

Omid Ashari provided the quotation in the title of this sub-chapter as he elaborated on the teacher's perspective on transformative education:

> My approach in my programme is that I always try to make the connection between who am I as a person or who I think I am and how do I want

to create impact, how do I want to influence based on business principles that we are providing. For me this is the entry point. So the starting point is a question, and this question in a liberal education is not teachable, needs to grow from within the person, the person needs to grow something and this growth which is induced in the learner is part of the answer. Because the answer is something that needs the evolution of one's consciousness, this grows and brings you to different thoughts which you could not have thought of. So the person needs to catapult herself or himself slowly into a certain direction. I use the same principles I want to convey and transmit to students first to myself. So basically, I teach myself. While I teach myself, I wake up the interests in students to also wake up this interest in them; it is not about teaching them but about developing them.

(interview, 2015)

Ashari, speaking from long-term experience as both teacher and programme director of the HSG master's in strategy and international management, which is explicitly designed to encourage transformative learning, made two important points: first, that to encourage transformative learning means to engage as a person with the persons being taught, and second, that what he saw as the main goal for transformative learning was 'not teachable' in the terms of a management education standard which relies on subject-based curricula. He told us, "You cannot direct change. It is like gardening, you create a momentum, otherwise it is not sustainable".

We asked Ashari about how these two aspects of transformative teaching were aligned with the highly competitive selection process that students have to go through before being admitted to the programme, a process which needs to adhere to recognisable standards—in order to be recognised by ranking agencies—and which thus must at least in part be influenced by techniques of instrumental teaching. He replied that, although there was indeed a strong element of the instrumental about this process (for example, the weight that BA grades carry for admission), part of the selection process was also designed so as to choose personalities who would be willing to engage in transformative learning. For him, students'

most important qualification is truthfulness, to have a desire to explore oneself, not saying "I am actually done as a person, I am finished, I just do this programme because it is a passport, brings me credibility, I take it with me and move on". A person who has a desire to improve but not for his/her own purposes, but because he or she wants to be able to contribute towards something, because she or he is not afraid to contribute towards something. If you lack selfconfidence, you do not want to be part of something, you want to be the boss, the one to [whom] everyone listens [. . .]. For me this is a signal of lack of selfconfidence. Self-confident people are those who say, "I was wrong and I want to learn, I want to improve myself". Students who have this desire, they are the right people I would be looking for. [. . .] For me the humanities and social sciences are not contributions to my programme but the definition of my programme.

(interview, 2015)

Ashari's remark on teaching himself while teaching students has a dimension which is not wholly covered by his engaging with students as a person; that is, the question of how exactly to go about transformative teaching practically when such teaching is not officially on the agenda of management education and not supported by the body of techniques and learning goals established for more traditional modes of teaching, which means that such techniques and learning goals are not easily accessible to teaching faculty even if they are willing to get involved with them. Highlighting the fact that academic teachers as such are seldom, if ever systematically trained in teaching techniques, since this is not an intrinsic part of their own academic education, and they thus acquire such techniques mostly by emulating their own teachers and developing their own individual aptitude, this question becomes all the more relevant in the context of a rather radical innovation like the transition from instrumental to transformative teaching.

Annemette Kjærgaard, when we asked about how she and her colleagues at CBS practised such teaching, told us frankly,

Exploring how to transform students, we want to do it, but we do not know how to do it. [. . .] It is not clear how to develop human quality in management education. These are aspects that are not currently extensively worked on.

(interview, 2014)

Teachers who do work on those aspects, like Kjærgaard and her colleague Sven Bislev, are therefore more or less left to their own devices when developing their approaches. Bislev explained to us that part of the reason for this was that the university as a whole seemed to shy away from the idea of fostering "human quality", especially in undergraduate education:

Educating is also a form of *Bildung*, education of your personality. However, we have not operationalised this aspect. What do we aim at? In which form do we build students' personalities? What is the aim of it? How much do we want to intervene? We need to get closer to that. We are getting closer to this type of education, closer to being concerned with the subjectivity of students. How do they perceive themselves, how do they accommodate the influences that come from us with their own life, background, inclinations, perception of the world? The traditional way of looking at it in economics is that everyone is supposed to be a rational person, so there is no reason in discussing this, because the choices people make are just an expression of their preferences that they wish to optimise. But in reality [this] is not empirically true. Decisions are made, actions are made, inclinations formed for all sort[s] of reasons. Those reasons are not permanent and change all the time, and are influenced by the social and cultural context. This complicated universe of ideas and actions is one way in which students' subjectivity encounters a large universe of meanings. We are not the ones necessarily shaping the minds of students, but we do have a role in it. We should be more conscious of our role and the effect we have.

(interview, 2014)

Bislev himself chooses to approach transformative teaching via the concept of subjectivity, as mentioned in his statement. For him, subjectivity is about "the relationship between emotions and understanding", a concept which is informed by sociology, psychology and literary studies, and which has the potential to address the "core problem of combining knowledge and action", leading the students away from the 'automated model' of rational choice towards

a much more nuanced and complicated view where action is a choice that is made on the basis not only of your knowledge but of the context and your maturity. We are human, not machines, cogs in a wheel. Subjectivity is where we do 'our things'.

(interview, 2014)

This concept, however, needs to be developed further in order to become systematically applicable in transformational teaching, as his ideas about it are still in a state of emergence:

We need to put words into this personal development trajectory, so we can discuss it in an intellectually qualified way. [. . .] We need to teach it in such a way that makes sense for students, in a way that they recognise [as] relevant for their education. [. . .] But it has not yet been reality-tested. It has to be unfolded, and I hope that students can appreciate it and recognise it.

(interview, 2014)

The reality of which Bislev talked, however, is determined not only by students' appreciation but also by the measurability of the learning outcomes of transformative teaching, and this remains a problem which is as yet unsolved. Tuija Nikko, quality manager in the Dean's Unit of the School of Business at Aalto University, stated,

The idea of the learner, of reflection, of critical thinking and creativity, all these diverse approaches to learning make it hard to establish learning goals and quality assurance, since professors are interested in developing students' capabilities, not in following an established set of learning objectives, which makes it difficult to assess.

(interview, 2015)

At the same time, as Edward Ashbee at CBS pointed out, there is, of course, also the factor of the resources available for teaching that should be considered in this context, that is, the question of whether "the expenditure of these resources is worth the objective" of interdisciplinary transformative teaching:

> We take many of these issues for granted, we do not take the time to reflect and think about these issues. Couldn't we just settle for being multidisciplinary? Isn't that good enough? [. . .] Given the fact [that] we have a limited amount of resources and staff, I think I would use those resources to do a better job in providing a multidisciplinary education, improving particular courses and giving answers to the issues that affect particular courses. This would be more useful than working on interdisciplinar[it]y.
>
> *(interview, 2014)*

From another perspective but with a similar emphasis on the question of resources, Bogdan Costea explained that the programmes offering integrated management education at LUMS have been and are being established without

> any significant cost for development and launching, since students join already existing courses. This means, on the one hand, that this strategy can achieve an easy buy-in from the organisation, and on the other hand, it means that 'integration' is done by the students. These new programmes are in fact repackaging of already developed courses.
>
> *(interview, 2015)*

In consequence, transformative teaching even at schools which actively pursue the integration of the humanities and social sciences remains a niche product, which in turn means that its outreach is usually limited to the comparatively few courses taught by faculty engaging with it, a circumstance which of course also limits its hopes for success. As Vincent Kaufmann, professor of French and media at the HSG School of the Humanities and Social Sciences and former chair of the Contextual Studies programme, put it,

> [I]t doesn't really make sense to reflect on Thursdays between 10 and 12 and learn by heart the rest of the week. The humanities are a reflection culture, and if the rest of the time is done the other way around, learning by heart, this is a major contradiction.
>
> *(interview, 2015)*

At the same time, even faculty who practise transformative teaching, like Florian Wettstein, professor of business ethics at the same school, who has his students read and perform Wolfram von Eschenbach's mediaeval romance *Parzival* (Wolfram, 2004), are reluctant to leave more traditional forms of teaching completely behind:

> I wouldn't say "All we should do from now on is theatre", there is still value in the established academic learning formats where we reflect, discuss, learn theories and so on. But new mixtures of modes of learning will be important. Transformational experiences are really important where we discuss openly values and positions. We, as professors, are probably hesitant to do this, and if we don't do this we cannot expect the students to do so. This is also tied to my identity as a researcher, which does not socialise you to think and practise in this way. You don't want to be 'the fluffy guy'.
>
> *(interview, 2015)*

For teaching and other faculty, therefore, there seem to be three major problems with transformative management education: the lack of available practical teaching techniques, including the definition of and procedures for the assessment of learning outcomes; the organisational difficulties in comprehensively establishing transformative and interdisciplinary education under conditions of limited institutional resources; and, finally, the image of 'fluffiness' or, as the students at CBS had it, 'vagueness' (interview, 2014), attached to teaching formats which cross the borders between traditional—and traditionally accepted—teaching formats and others which work towards opening up students for reflection using methods derived from the humanities and social sciences, especially since that image carries a stigma implying that the latter methods are of little, if any, applicable practical value to future managers.

"There Is No Gap Between Theory and Practice": The Role of Professional Practice in Academic Management Education

Asked about the relationship between transformative teaching and professional practice in academic management education, Lucas Introna, professor in the Department of Organisation, Work and Technology at LUMS, told us that, in his eyes, the idea of practice as such underlying this question was decidedly questionable, since students in fact came to the school with lots of practical experience:

> There is no gap between theory and practice; they've all lived in a family and they have life experience; let them reflect about basic questions: if I gave you a million, what would you do? They have the wrong idea that management is that miracle tool-box, out of this comes the experience to

say, "Gimme that secret knowledge!" But even the senior managers think so, they believe that I can master my mastery by knowing the knowledge.

(interview, 2015)

The idea of practice informing Introna's comment is a wide one, tying in with much of the input on the shift from subject- or teacher-centred education to student-centred education that was presented in the first part of this chapter. Introna defined practical experience as the everyday experience that students bring to university and go on accumulating there both inside and outside their courses. As every student—and every faculty member, for that matter—is *a priori* immersed in practice via their social existence as such, Introna claimed that social and professional practice are not so categorically different from each other that the latter could be sufficiently isolated from the former, so as then to devise a concrete body of knowledge to be mastered for the one without paying attention to the other; instead, the practical experience that students bring with them should be drawn upon as a valuable resource for the mastering of a holistic concept of management.

Introna was seconded in this thought by his colleague at LUMS Laurence Hemming, professor of philosophy, who explained that management education was seen by many students as a kind of general education extending and elaborating on what the liberal arts used to offer, that is, an education in how to act within society as a whole, which today is very much shaped by concerns related directly or indirectly to business and management issues. This means that students who enter a management school expect to acquire a certain kind of performative training:

It's a classic notion of the Greek educated person—the *epist[ēmos]*, the one who knows his way around, who can conduct him- or herself with decorum and propriety in the *agora*, the temple and the battlefield. [...] It's exactly what happens in management schools: the students will learn the technologies to conduct her- or himself with decorum on the battlefield, which maybe means in front of the spreadsheet and in the management meeting.

(interview, 2015)

These technologies can either be learned instrumentally, donned and shed at will like a working outfit designed for use as the professional occasion may arise, or they can be acquired transformatively, meaning that students reflect on their acquisition as a process of personal evolution which enables them to meet far more than merely the challenges of a specialised job profile, namely the challenges inherent in a societal development which has long since started to blur the line between professional and individual lives, and, especially due to the communication patterns engendered by digital media, is likely to continue doing so. According to Hemming, this constitutes a chance for innovation in management education which management schools have yet to recognise, as they are still caught up in the artificial separation of theory from practice, and vice versa, which lies at the bottom of the conflict between those who clamour for more practical skills in management school graduates and those who insist rather on having them engage with critical thinking and similar reflective practices during their studies.

Asked about what precisely he saw as the added value of academic education for professional practice, since such a wide concept of practice could as such surely not be constrained to universities, Lucas Introna laid down a very clear demarcation line between academic teaching and learning through practical experiences: "One thing we do is to teach how to reflect; practitioners don't reflect!" (interview, 2015). In context, this was said less to denigrate practitioners' ability to reflect as such and more to outline the effect that the concept of professional practice projected by educators preferring instrumental teaching has on the image of management carried by students—and thus on their willingness to engage with transformative learning. This image defines practical work as being far removed from the assumedly theoretical exercise of reflection, instead of recognising reflection as a mode with which to enhance practical work. Introna, however, sees the value of academic management education precisely in teaching students to apply reflection practically. He deems it problematic that "universities build 'editors' in each and every student; they provide for parameters how to judge the world", whereas universities' real duty, based on the Humboldtian paradigm of *Bildung*, is to teach students to reflect critically on the frameworks of values that they are working on and, instead of judging reality on the grounds of predefined criteria learned by heart, to reach individually reasoned decisions in their practical work, decisions for which they are able and willing to take responsibility.

The concept of reflection was throughout very much at the forefront of what our interviewees saw as the contribution of the humanities and social sciences to management education. Kristian Kreiner, then-director of the Centre for Management Studies of the Building Process at CBS, told us that students usually had little or "no clues [about] the implications of their knowledge for management", as they worked mainly on the "assumption of rational decision-making", favouring productivity over creativity and thus failing to meet the complexity of practical work:

> To be able to tell people what to do, you need to define a very narrow scope of interest and this [is] not practical, because the conditions under which that advice is true are far too narrow.
>
> *(interview, 2014)*

Sven Bislev, the CBS vice-dean for education, elaborated further, emphasising again his notion that to develop what he called the subjectivity of students might be a viable way of bridging the perceived gap between theory and practice:

> Our main focus is in educating students to work in organised environments, influence the environments, take part in decision-making, operate steering

and governance systems of organisations. However, there is an ambivalence, because these practical[ly] oriented aims have to be delivered with a research background, using scientific tools, scientific forms of reflection. We can see an in-built contradiction between practice and analysis. So I am trying to conceptualise practice to outline the different meanings of the concept, so far, I have got three: to be oriented towards action (instrumentality), to study how action happens (familiarity with the fields of action), to analyse all sort[s] of empirical things. [. . .] Any businessmen can say some buzz-words about what [. . .] business [is] about. Currently, a lot of external examin[er]s come from practice, and professors can have a hard time explaining to these professionals that theories are relevant and necessary for analysis. Many managers have simplified notions, fashionable concepts, phrases that they think are good enough for taking decisions on a lot of things. Trying to formulate how practice comes into academic learning [. . .], developing students' personality or students' subjectivity could be a helpful concept.

(interview, 2014)

The image of professional practice underlying these considerations is based on the notion that the gap mentioned earlier derives from the mistaken idea that theories have nothing to do with the reality of the labour market, while in fact teachers like Bislev view them as essential to deal with this reality.

At Aalto University's School of Business, bridging this gap is part of the reason why it was decided to enter into close collaboration with the School of Arts, such collaboration being perceived as offering an efficiently practical approach to reshaping management education. As Mikko Koria, then-professor of practice in the Department of Management Studies (today he teaches at the Institute for Design Innovation at Loughborough University in London), explained to us, the school, though not explicitly engaging with the humanities and social sciences as such, had decided to focus on the concrete situatedness of management practice, providing "epistemological flexibility by bringing in different approaches and methods from the social sciences", because they understood such practice as being interdisciplinary *per se*, so that teaching only disciplinary skills did and could not meet the needs of students:

> There is a strong network of professors from practice that have strong relationships with organisations, and their approach is interdisciplinary. It seems to me they have perceived the risk of this practice-based approach and are investing strongly in research to overcome being perceived as a vocational school.

(interview, 2015)

Running the International Design Business Management programme (IDBM) at the Aalto School of Business as its director, Koria understands the challenge of teaching management as that of "teaching different disciplines to work together". In his eyes, epistemological flexibility, that is, the ability to reframe problems reflectively using methodologies from different disciplines as and when the problem to be solved demands them, is the most important skill to be imparted to management students, not least because this is what future employers will expect of them, in his experience:

> Companies would benefit extremely because they would not have to train people on [an] *ad hoc* basis. Companies do not train people for interdisciplinary collaboration, but nevertheless ask employees to work interdisciplinarily, which probably is highly ineffective.
>
> *(interview, 2015)*

Koria's IDBM programme has students of management, students of engineering and other technologies and students of art and design work together on a concrete problem being put to them by practitioners. The ensuing discussions teach students first and foremost both to try to explain their own approach to the issues in question and to understand the approach of the other disciplines, since at the start they tend to take the ontological legitimacy of their own disciplinary knowledge for granted and thus have to learn to question it with a view to finding a solution as a team. The point provoking the most heated discussions in this context, Koria has observed, is the question of how to optimise the product that they are asked to develop:

> It boils down to optimisation: how do you optimise? Engineers usually optimise for a single best solution, they believe very firmly that there is a best technical solution. Business people on the other hand say, "Well, fine, there might be a best technical solution but that may not be the best solution business-wise", so they optimise for money, which means that you might use the second-best technology for the market, but then the designer doesn't think like that at all, he thinks about the optimisation for affect, for the feeling. So the designer understands "there is no best solution, there are a million solutions, and we choose the one that has the best emotional impact".
>
> *(interview, 2015)*

In the course of the programme, the students' practical work is accompanied by group reflections on the process as well as individual coaching sessions. The goal of the programme is to educate them towards becoming what Koria called an "umbrella type" of manager, that is, a manager who is able not only to conduct but also to orchestrate interdisciplinary team-work efficiently, as he or she has learned not only to do but also systematically to reflect on his or her professional activities, which means that reflection is in fact taught as a means effectively to enhance practical productivity.

A similar idea informs the Contextual Studies programme at HSG, even though, because it is not so much a programme like Koria's IDBM but rather a general education offered to all students of the university alongside their core studies, it operates in less project-oriented terms. However, the notion that reflection improves rather than hinders professional practice is, as Chris Steyaert, professor of organisational psychology and a member of both the School of Management and the School of Humanities and Social Sciences at HSG, told us, very much the linchpin of what he saw as the educational goal of contextual studies:

> The official story is still that we do both rigour and relevance, and I always say that these do not work without reflection. You can't do rigour without reflection, and you can never do relevance without reflection as you are always relevant for someone or something and not for somebody else. There is a lot of managerialism at this university which has to be questioned, of course, but the questioning can also be done in a reflexive way so you don't play the 'anti-management' position which is not very fruitful.
>
> *(interview, 2015)*

The way Steyaert put this hints at the fact that even, and perhaps especially, at business universities which have been engaging in integrated management education for a long time, while there is a basic agreement on favouring the transformational instead of the instrumental approach to teaching, there is also much discussion on how to go about it and what role the humanities and social sciences can or should play. While Steyaert turns the issue of reflection back on such discussions, opting for mediating dialogue between management and con-textual studies instead of principle-driven confrontation, there are also voices which doubt that the humanities and social sciences can have much, if any, impact on the practical side of management education. The most critical vote in that respect was cast by Simon Evenett, professor of economics at HSG and in charge of the HSG's MBA, who told us that, at least in the realm of executive education, while not contesting that the humanities and social sciences might in fact have something to offer as such, he did not see them engaging with practice on any level:

> Many students do an MBA to figure out what they want to do. We do have a very elaborate development of personal competencies, that starts with reflection, which aims at opening their minds to different opportunities and possibilities. We do not use any humanities professors for this work. [. . .] All too often my social sciences and humanities colleagues think that know-ing is enough, and they do not understand that doing is important, it is a

pre-requirement for becoming what they want to become. This is where my colleagues fall down. They do not understand the importance of doing.

(interview, 2015)

As will be seen in the next chapter, Evenett was not alone in criticising teachers in the humanities and social sciences for their lack of willingness, if not ability, to engage actively with issues that are important to management education. The point here, however, is mainly that he seemed to perceive 'doing' to be more or less categorically out of the range of the humanities' and social sciences' field of expertise, an attitude which is shared by many students at HSG. Ulrich Schmid, professor of Russian at the HSG School of Humanities and Social Sciences, summed this up by referring to the surveys that HSG regularly conducts among their graduates:

> One-third of graduates thinks contextual studies are great. One-third does [not] care but does not oppose them either. One-third thinks it is chicanery. This is pretty much also the reaction distribution I get in the seminars. My ambition is to get the two-thirds who are not interested to engage and free them from their intellectual cage they are in—in my opinion—which is already visible in their criticism expecting instrumental knowledge.
>
> *(interview, 2015)*

For Schmid, the dissemination of transformational knowledge was both the main added value and the main duty of academic management education. To educate students on the assumption that all they need in professional practice is a tool-box of instrumental knowledge therefore means to give up on the character of the university oriented towards holistic *Bildung* as developed by Humboldt and his peers:

> If you really think along these lines, we should immediately drop reading Goethe at school. We should never give up on *Bildung*. If we do, we become a Faculty of Applied Science; then we are no longer a university and it would not be clear how we would be different from an in-house training session in a bank.
>
> *(interview, 2015)*

Teaching instrumental knowledge of the type that Schmid associated with an "in-house training session in a bank" seems insufficient for satisfying the demands either of future employers or of society as a whole. SMU, among the schools we visited perhaps the one most explicitly connecting its strategic efforts to integrate the humanities and social sciences into management education to such demands, launched their task force "humanities@smu" expressly with a view to meeting educational needs which had evolved beyond the tool-boxes offered by more traditional management education. Francis Koh, professor of economics at SMU, and at the time we visited, its provost, pointed out that, ever since its foundation, SMU has been closely attuned to what its stakeholders expect of it:

> We produce with a purpose in mind in our education system. We produce to the industry. [. . .] The educational system is seen as a system of supply to the workforce and educational investment is all about shaping this. [. . .] Education is meant to prepare you for the work force.
>
> *(interview, 2014)*

Therefore, the main goal of the reform that the "humanities@smu" task force was pursuing was to increase the employability of their graduates, as Sriven Naidu, director of the task force, explained,

> SMU has reached a stage where we can no longer sell our education offer on the basis of good salaries achieved by graduates. We perform well in this regard, but our alumni now begin to reach the age level where corporate-level positions begin to be relevant. We now need to think more about how we perform in relation to delivering 'c-level' competencies. This is also an important background for thinking about the strategy 2025—how to educate towards c-level carriers? In this context, the expansion of humanities is important.
>
> *(interview, 2014)*

This expansion was intended to add skills like reflection and critical thinking to the portfolio of abilities needed to meet the challenges of the growing complexity of professional practice. As Francis Koh put it, this meant that business schools simply had no choice other than to adjust their curricula accordingly: "If the industry wants candidates that can handle complexity, they need to see business schools deliver on this" (interview, 2014).

All in all, two key aspects stand out in the material that we collected on the issue of the functional connection between the shift towards transformational teaching and the humanities' and social sciences' contribution to management education. The first aspect is an apparently broad consensus that the reflective knowledge the humanities and social sciences provide is not only perceived to be the main source of transformational dynamics, but also that this knowledge is mostly seen to be directly related to—and thus to impact on—the way in which academic management education trains students for professional practice. This finding squarely contradicts the clichéd notion that humanities and social science knowledge is mostly theoretical in nature and thus of no use for practitioners, while at the same time highlighting that there might well be an equally clichéd notion of professional practice informing instrumental concepts of management education. The second aspect concerns the image of academic management education as, by dint of being academic, *a priori* less concerned with professional practice than with the research-based construction of theories. Since each school we visited works closely with practitioners from business and industry on several levels, beginning with employing them as part-time teaching faculty and bringing them together with students in projects and career fairs, up to and including involving them in their advisory and governing boards, there is little warrantable reason to suspect these schools of losing touch with practice. However, there is a growing awareness in management schools that they might have to put serious conceptual effort into translating the relationship between theory and practice, as it is understood and indeed practised by them, into terms that are both understandable and acceptable to practitioners. The gap between theory and practice still dominating the perception of academic management education seems to be not so much an effect of practitioners' inability to reflect but rather of the momentum that the 'academicising' of management education has developed in terms of over-emphasising the scholarly and the theoretical to the detriment of practical knowledge.

"Knowledge You Can't Google": Practices of Teaching Integrated Management Education

For once we chose a quotation for the title of a sub-chapter which does not directly derive from our interviews but instead from a book chapter (albeit one whose authors we interviewed when we visited CBS), since the formula "knowledge you can't Google" simply cannot be beaten in its descriptive precision for the content of transformative teaching. In their chapter, "Knowledge You Can't Google: Teaching Philosophy at the Business School", Rasmus Johnsen, Morten Sørensen Thaning and Michael Pedersen (2016) suggest a pedagogical approach towards transformative education based on their own teaching experience, which focuses on questions rather than answers, the learning goal being the fostering of four competences:

> First, the capacity to analyse and evaluate the assumptions that construct management and organization as cultural practices enables our students to see business as embedded in society. Second, the ability to articulate the fundamental values and problems that are at stake within business practice and knowledge allows them to work with such values within a wider historical and cultural horizon. Third, the competence to communicate knowledge of such values and problems in a vocabulary that focuses on questioning and diagnosis, rather than directly on solutions, encourages the students to take the freedom to step back from their professional practice and reflect on it in cooperation with others. Finally, these competences all comprise part of the ability to contribute to a discussion about different courses of practical action in light of philosophical analyses and arguments.
>
> *(Johnsen et al., 2016, p. 384)*

As Johnsen told us (interview, 2016), the encoding of these competences reflects the format and results of a workshop based on peer-coaching teachers entitled "The Business of Teaching" that he ran for the first time in June 2016, at CBS, in co-operation with several business schools in the US (Franklin and Marshall College, New York University Stern, Santa Clara University and Washington and Lee University) and in Europe (SSE, HSG and the University of Essex), and with the help of William Sullivan, one of the authors of the Carnegie report of 2011, and Claire Preisser, from the Aspen Institute's Business and Society programme. The workshop focused on content which students could not learn more efficiently through practical work within the same time-span as their course-work, seeking to define the added value of academic education, as opposed to the 'learning by doing' approach, by encouraging teachers to have students engage in discussion about questions which have no predefined answers, up to and including the questioning of the frameworks of management education as such.

During our site visits we found many courses which were taught on similar principles. One of them was the "Global Integrative Module" co-established and co-taught by Anna Iñesta, director of the Center for Educational Innovation at ESADE (see http://itemsweb.esade.edu/dipqa/GIM/ebook2/index.html). Designed for first-year students, the development of the Global Integrative Module was funded by the Management Education for Tomorrow Fund of the Graduate Management Admission Council, and it was run for the first time in 2014. The course charges student teams with developing answers to the question, "What can companies contribute to reduce economic inequality in the world?" by examining companies, government agencies and even business schools of their choice, at the end presenting a paper which contains concrete recommendations for the examined objects, as Iñesta explained:

> What we ask them to do is to produce a paper that needs to have the fundamentals of a conceptualisation, they have their sources, websites, e.g. and then they have to choose which companies they want to analyse. So they have to go and interview someone from that company in order to see what they're doing.
>
> *(interview, 2015)*

The student teams are assembled from different business schools—NYU, Bocconi, Sogang Business School in South Korea and ESADE—and from both BA and MA programmes, so as to provide maximum diversity, adding the challenge of working from different time zones to the mix. Put under intense time pressure to produce a viable concept, students, as Iñesta told us, often found themselves under a level of stress which comes as a shock to them, being challenged at once intellectually, emotionally and technically. The role of faculty in this is not, as Iñesta put it, that of the "sage-on-the-stage", but rather that of a facilitator, pointing out problems, keeping the research on track and providing feedback and individual coaching as needed. During the whole time, students are encouraged to reflect openly on their experiences, and in the end, they are asked to evaluate what was most difficult for them and why. Part of the support that faculty offer is expertise drawn from the humanities and social sciences, up to and including recommendations of literature such as, for instance, works of Shakespeare if pertinent to the project, with the result that, as Iñesta explained, students through the combination of practical experience and in-depth reflection often found it surprisingly easy to connect such expertise to the problems they encountered and thus ended up being very appreciative of this input.

A similar approach of drastically reframing the learning situation of students is practised by Chris Steyaert, professor of organisational psychology at the HSG School of Management, and Timon Beyes, professor of design, innovation and aesthetics at the Department of Management, Politics and Philosophy at CBS, in their course "Cities and Creativity". Steyaert and Beyes established this MA course some years ago at HSG, where it has meanwhile become a very successful part of the Contextual Studies programme. The course sends students into urban spaces, having them walk through them in order to expose themselves, physically and emotionally, to different atmospheres and urban spaces, thus moving through the city and mapping atmospheres and their own reactions to them. In a kick-off session they are briefed in relevant ethnographic methodology—descriptive mapping, mental mapping, psycho-geographical mapping—which they are then asked to apply to their experiences when walking through the city over several days, putting their experiences into writing as well as into a series of photographs taken over these days. Teaching faculty support students as facilitators during this time, leaving the student teams walking alone but being always on call (by mobile) so as to join students when and if they need advice or they ask for reflection on what they find. The idea behind the course concept is to encourage transformative education through what Steyaert called "embodied learning", since

> embodied learning makes students alive. This is perhaps the most important outcome of learning, not the grades. And there is some psychological element in this. Being alive means to become trustful in your insecurity, trustful that you can do something that is not known. We talk so much about entrepreneurship and creativity, new things and change. I find it very important to embrace the possibility of doing things differently. This is a very realistic, not idealistic, ambition for a learning outcome.
>
> *(interview, 2015)*

"Transformative Humanities?" Conclusions and Suggestions

Seen in the light of the findings we have presented, there can be little doubt that the business schools we visited throughout are committed to management education as a transforming practice rather than as a distribution of instrumental tool-boxes. The transition from the latter to the former, however, is not a smooth one, placing students and teachers in a field of tension which is rather difficult to navigate for both parties. Overall, there is a broadly shared impression that traditional management education was and still is acting on the basis of a philosophy of instrumental education, that is, an education aiming first and foremost at imparting skills as tools to be used. Integrating the humanities and social sciences, on the other hand, is perceived as departing from this tradition in two possible directions. One, the more moderate one, is a spin-off of the instrumental philosophy, adding disciplines to the curricular mix which have not been part of the classical set up, which might be—and sometimes indeed is—seen as an incremental add-on with its own instrumental value. The other and more radical direction and that which most of our sample group of business schools favoured, is to change the nature of management education fundamentally by integrating those disciplines, replacing the instrumental with a more transformative approach with their help.

While tension between the old and the new, between solidly secure tradition and the as yet uncharted waters of innovational practice, is more or less a general phenomenon in the realm of organisational change management, it seems that integrating the humanities and social sciences into management education adds an element to this tension which to some extent heightens it above the ordinary. This element is the impact that humanities and social science methodologies have on transformative education, an impact which is due to their being a "culture of reflection", as Vincent Kaufmann at HSG put it (interview, 2015), a culture which not only is itself operating along transformational lines but, more pertinently, provides the techniques that Mezirow described as the mainstays of transformative learning (Mezirow, 1981, p. 5) to other disciplines. One of the most striking phrases in this context was coined by Annemette Kjærgaard, vice-dean of learning at CBS, who used the term "transformative humanities" in our interview with her, as opposed to the "plain science" of instrumental skills which could be learned by rote (interview, 2014).

Where humanities and social sciences are integrated into management education, three major lines of conflict appear between the instrumental and the transformative approaches. One is a conflict between students' expectations and preconceptions of management education on the one hand—which rather tend towards the instrumental—and the goals and practices of transformative education on the other, especially if and when the latter engages with disciplines from the humanities and social sciences which are considered by students as not forming an intrinsic part of management studies. Another conflict line runs between the usually rather passionate commitment of teachers engaging with transformative education and the fact that they have not received or do not even have access to systematic training in this type of education, while the organisational structures from which they operate are not easily compatible with the teaching formats they develop, so that, for both students and teachers, the costs of opportunity for such practices are significantly higher than those for the more traditional set up. Lastly, the understanding of professional practice plays a role in management education which might bear some critical examining in the light of the question as to whether or not the humanities and social sciences can contribute to students' practical training. On these three issues, we will now offer our conclusions from the material presented as well as a number of suggestions about how to defuse these conflicts.

Students' Perspective: Start With the First Year

How much exactly students can be transformed, and how far being transformed through academic management education impacts on the mind-set they bring to their studies, is hard to gauge. Where data are available, as, for example, in the excellent study of Ragnhild Kvålshaugen (2001) on the relation between education and practice in the professional lives of Norwegian managers, they point to students being not much susceptible to formation, instead rather viewing management education as the entry point into a prosperous career and going through it to achieve their goal with pragmatic determination. Based on data collected by the US Higher Education Research Institute, as quoted by the Carnegie report, management students after graduation are also significantly less interested in questions as to the meaning of human existence, the relevance of their chosen professional field to society, or the understanding of different cultural contexts than, for example, students of the humanities and social sciences, instead firmly prioritising questions as to how high their entry salaries should be and how to work towards cumulating wealth for themselves (Colby et al., 2011, p. 42). That means, as the authors state, that "[t]o some extent, the differences between business and arts and sciences students are already present when students come to college, but majoring in business during college certainly does not erase those differences" (2011, p. 42; see also Pascarella & Terenzini, 2005). To opt for a transformative approach therefore means to work on and with students' expectations of and assumptions about management education as a whole.

Judging from our material as well as from published literature, transformative learning is not generally part of those expectations and assumptions. In one of his later works, Mezirow describes five ways to achieve transformation through learning:

> [R]eflecting critically on the source, nature and consequences of relevant assumptions—our own and those of others; in instrumental learning, determining that something is true (is as it is purported to be) by using empirical research methods; in communicative learning, arriving at more justified beliefs by participating freely and fully in an informed continuing discourse; taking action on our transformed perspective—we make a decision and live what we have come to believe until we encounter new evidence [. . .]; acquiring a disposition—to become more critically reflective of our own assumptions and those of others, to seek validation of our transformative

insights through more freely and fully participating in discourse and to follow through on our decision to act upon a transformed insight.

(Mezirow, 2009, p. 94)

Of these five ways, only critical reflection, more often encoded as critical thinking, has made it into the mainstream of management education, to the extent that it is referred to not only in literature on management education but also by practically all of its stakeholders inside and outside academia as being one of the most important skills for management students to acquire during their studies. Concepts like Kolb's "Learning Cycle" (1984) and Schön's "Reflective Practitioner" (1983; see also Schön, 1992) have accordingly been taken up appreciatively by many management educators.

Students, however, do not usually seem to share this appreciation. As several studies have shown, students tend to take reflection mostly for a tool that enables them to think about themselves and not as a tool to test suppositions and assumptions against evidence (Beveridge et al., 2013). If forced to practise it, they go through with it in the manner of a purely academic exercise, while not really seeing its added value for their professional lives (Duke & Appleton, 2000, p. 1565). Also, it obviously worries students to write and talk about issues they are uncertain about, hesitating to engage emotionally because they regard affective reflection as unprofessional (Platzer et al., 2000; Dyment & O'Connell, 2010; Dyment & O'Connell, 2011) and, when they are assessed for their reflective abilities through essay-writing, for example, they opt for opportunism towards the assumed assessment criteria instead of honestly questioning existing thoughts and practices (Maloney et al., 2013). Recent research suggests that this may well be due to the hold that instrumental modes of learning, experienced by students before they entered management education, still retain on them. If their previous education "had not encouraged them to think critically or to reflect", having trained them in "rote learning" so that they have "not been encouraged to think or discover things for themselves" (Platzer et al., 2000, p. 1004), critical reflection is obviously far more difficult to inspire by teaching than if students—distinctly in the minority in the sample group—have had some prior experience with it.

From what we have gathered, the results of this research apply to our sample group as well. In this context, it is noteworthy that the students to whom we talked not once related to their professional goals—and thus to their reason for studying at a business school—by expressing much interest or passion for the subject they were studying. Where there was passion, it was reserved for extracurricular activities like joining student clubs or the Student Union or, as in the case of Isak at SSE, for curating the school's art-work. Management as such, however, while specific courses or topics can elicit enthusiasm, seems not to be perceived as a subject matter which in and of itself attracted those studying it, while in our experience students for example of medicine and other natural sciences are much more explicitly interested in their subjects as such. Accordingly, the professional goals of management students are not so much couched in terms of how to become a good manager but rather in terms of how to become a successful entrepreneur or consultant or high-ranking, c-level executive, reflecting clearly their instrumental approach to management education. This hints at a systemic rather than a content-related effect shaping this approach which is specific to management education and, possibly, to management as a profession and which thus might bear examination on a much broader level than the one to which our report can aspire.

Viewing our interviewees' input in the light of Mezirow's theory, one way to go about changing the habit of thinking about management education in instrumental terms on the part of the students would be to transform their perspective on management education actively and from the very moment they enter the university. In other words, the success of perspective transformation through education in the way Mezirow advocates (2009) depends first and foremost on students being made aware of the fact that they are bringing a set preconception of what management education is about to their respective business schools, a preconception which is shaped before they even walk onto campus for the first time. Only when this awareness is created proactively and programmatically can students realistically be expected to engage with transformative learning practices, since to be prepared to be taken out of their comfort zone they must learn to face the fact that they have one in the first place and the fact that, at least in part, this zone is defined by beliefs and impressions which may not have much in common with reality.

Another reason for starting to expose students to transformative education as early as possible is that this type of education is processual by nature, "a movement through time of reforming reified structures of meaning by reconstructing dominant narratives" (Mezirow et al., 2000, p. 19). In other words, students need to be introduced to the notion that their whole education is a process of transformation which does not end with the final exam of any given course. This understanding is deeply at odds with the modular architecture of academic education as crystallised in the Bologna reform, since the latter operates on the logic of the incremental collection of skills imparted in course-shaped bits and pieces, which further explains why students find it so difficult to relate to transformative modes of teaching.

Therefore, ideally it would be in the first year of their studies that students should be confronted with the basics of transformative education for the first time. A possible way in which to go about this would be a mandatory introduction to management education, taught by a team of educators from different disciplines, which explicitly challenges students to explore their attitudes towards management and management education, to formulate their expectations in relation to both their personal and their professional development goals and to understand the relationship between management and society. This introductory course would be designed to make students aware of the fact that their approach to management is shaped by a set of values and experiences which are located in a specific cultural framework, to recognise and to critique the agendas in this framework and to develop a reflective individual position towards them. To evaluate students' progress, such a course would employ exploratory examination formats like learning diaries, group blogs and similar tools, the learning goals being (a) the ability for team-work and group learning and (b) the ability to distinguish between different frames of reference for problem-solving. The most important learning goal, however, would be for the students (c) to gain a first holistic image of what management education is or could be all about, enabling them to place their future studies into a context which, besides the utility of skills, allows them to develop a clear purpose for pursuing these studies towards the common good.

What this purpose could or should be is, as Laurent A. Parks Daloz puts it, "a hoary and honorable question" (Daloz, 2000, p. 118). In the light of the importance that the issue of sustainability and, on a broader level, the call for a more ethical approach to management overall has developed over recent decades, answering this question opens up two possible avenues to pursue. One is for teachers to agitate for—or, more discreetly, make space for students to agitate for—specific social changes, as Paulo Freire advocates (Freire, 1970). The other is for teachers to restrict themselves "to fostering general intellectual growth [. . .], assuming that such growth will lead to socially responsible choices" (Daloz, 2000, pp. 118–19; see also Kegan, 1982, 2009; Kohlberg, 1984). Mezirow and his followers clearly vote for the latter avenue, and indeed this seems to be rather more in line than the former with the academic freedom of research and teaching on the strength of which students are to be taught to reach their own conclusions about the problems with which they are confronted by teachers. Seen from this perspective, the overall purpose for students to develop could be based on their critical awareness of the fact that management theories and skills usually come with agendas shaped by the historical background, social connections and individual interests of their inventors, thus empowering them to set their own agenda in terms of critical reflection on their own background, connections and interests—which asks that teachers meet a very different set of challenges than those to which they are traditionally used.

Teachers' Perspective: Dialogical Interaction and 'Presencing'

"Educators of adults are in a unique position among professionals in that they often have not had the opportunity to learn how to do their job", Cranton and King state decisively at the beginning of an article entitled "Transformative Learning as a Professional Development Goal" (Cranton & King, 2003, p. 31). It is indeed one of the more astonishing aspects of academic education that those who are entrusted with it rarely have even the most rudimentary, if any training in teaching, usually being thrown into it to sink or swim, since such training is not yet compulsory for an academic career. This means that much of the didactic knowledge which shapes academic teaching is transmitted by implication rather than by design, leaving academic teaching faculty to develop "habits of mind" (Cranton & King, 2003, p. 33) about teaching more or less accidentally, habits which then are seldom reflected upon consciously (see also Wade & Yarbrough, 1996). As long as these habits are embedded in a teaching culture which is pre-stabilised by time-honoured traditions, they are easily sustainable, especially since academia tends to place the importance of research above that of teaching, but as our material shows, they are insufficient to meet the challenges of transformative education.

Transformative education asks a lot from teachers, even when it mainly sticks to the reflective practices that Mezirow advocates without venturing into the more psychological, spiritual and political spheres of holistic education suggested by Boyd (Boyd & Myers, 1988; Boyd, 1991), Freire (1970) and Dirkx (1998, 2003). Traditionally, the role of the teacher is that of imparting information and giving directions about what to do with it. This role is strictly hegemonic, implying that the teacher is in charge by virtue of his or her superior access to privileged information which is doled out according to his or her choices both in terms of content and in terms of didactics. Transformative education is a wholly different kettle of fish, expecting teachers to enter into a 'learning partnership' (Swanson, 2010) with their students whereby they engage with them on a more personal level, without, or at least with much less of the shelter that traditional student-teacher hierarchies provide. Lacking formal training in teaching in the first place, many teachers, for instance, find themselves overtaxed by students' demands for the feedback that is necessary to foster reflection in dialogue (Dyment & O'Connell, 2010; Dyment & O'Connell, 2011; Boud, 1999), and this in turn means that, in the words of Omid Ashari at HSG, teachers basically have to teach themselves when they turn to transformative education (interview, 2015).

The quality of teaching currently is not only hotly debated by student unions at business schools but reverberates throughout the academic landscape for two reasons. Firstly, the Bologna reform has been implemented by most universities in a way that has resulted in a far heavier load of course-work for students than before, making them extremely sensitive to the way in which teachers do or do not help them carry that load. The second reason is the fundamental change imposed on academic teaching by the omnipresent availability of digitalised information, the effects of which clash brutally with the traditional classroom teaching formats that were mainly dedicated to imparting information to students. In the era of Google, Wikipedia and open access publishing, a huge part of the knowledge that once used to be the sole property of academia, making it necessary to attend university bodily to partake of it, is easily retrieved and processed by means of computers, smartphones and other electronic equipment almost everywhere, a state of affairs which applies to the basics of management education as well as to any other discipline.

For students, it therefore no longer makes sense to sit through endless *ex cathedra* lectures on established methods or other long-codified contents when they can find the necessary data by Googling them and can then process them comfortably at home or wherever they choose, especially when, as is often the case in large classes, they are talked *to* rather than *with*. They find it increasingly frustrating to be served information in class, to be expected to gobble it up as fast and comprehensively as they can and to spit it out again, more or less undigested, at exam time, a mechanism that we have repeatedly heard described as 'bulimic learning'. What students look for instead is what Johnsen, Thaning and Pedersen so aptly dub "knowledge you can't Google" (2016): a kind of knowledge which relies on direct personal human interaction for its transmission, making classroom experiences worth the students' time by means of a "dialogic, relationally oriented pedagogy" (Lysaker & Furuness, 2011, p. 183).

In developing such a pedagogy, teachers will have to meet two different, if related, challenges. For one thing, they will have to restructure the knowledge they are used to imparting *ex cathedra* in terms of reflective interaction with their students, some examples of which we have showcased earlier. This certainly need not happen at the cost of canonical content, far from it; rather, it means offering this content in a way that students can absorb through its critical reframing, ideally in a manner that has them recreate it by fully understanding its frameworks of reference in relation to themselves. The effects of digitalisation will be of considerable help here, allowing, through blended learning and flipped-classroom teaching, more time to be spent in the classroom on interaction, always provided that digital formats of teaching are employed not as replacements but as complementary devices (Bachmann & Shah, 2016).

The second challenge is perhaps more difficult to meet, because it involves the teacher more personally. Many students feel that their direct interaction with teachers is insufficient for their—the students'—needs, there being too little of it and what there is being conducted too perfunctorily on the teacher's side. This is most marked where they wish for thorough feedback on presentations and exams but also in view of the teacher's overall attitude, which is often perceived by students to be routinely distant. It is difficult to tell exactly how much of this attitude is due to overwork—and indeed, seeing the disproportion between student and teaching faculty numbers at most schools we visited, there is much legitimate cause for this—and how much, on the other hand, is due to the "habits of mind" mentioned earlier (Cranton & King, 2003), based on an implicit understanding that the hierarchical boundaries dividing teachers and students must not be crossed. Transformative teaching, however, needs the teacher to engage rather closely with his or her students, possibly and even probably taking the teacher out of his or her comfort zone just as effectively as the students. Developing a concept for this could be based on what the MIT scholar Claus Otto Scharmer calls "presencing" (Scharmer, 2016). A hybrid term fusing the words 'presence' and 'sensing', "presencing" means programmatically to attach importance to the here and now of students'—and teachers'—presence in the classroom, both in terms of the intellectual experience of being in a situation where individual history is shaped towards the future, by a team, and the sensual experience of being close to and interacting with other bodily present persons.

Departing from the notion that the humanities and social sciences could and should account for much of both the method and the content of transformational teaching, this means that the concept of presencing could create an ideal interface for the translation of its type of knowledge not only into the theoretical but also into the practical professional training of management students. As the material we presented in the third part of this chapter shows, there seemed to be a clear consensus throughout the schools we visited that they have to offer a lot to professional practice, especially in the area of critical reflection, which is unanimously seen as the most important skill they are able to teach. Extending the lines sketched out in this material and connecting them to the division of educational labour between a mostly digital imparting of information and the co-operation on its critical digestion in presencing mode, the humanities and social sciences could help to reduce the gap between theory and practice by which their competences usually are judged through linking group learning processes to a transformational understanding of management. This understanding would focus on tapping into the potential for relational problem-solving that is inherent in the social and cultural embeddedness of the human being, placing the acquisition of necessary professional skills in its broader context by bringing this embeddedness to life through relational teaching.

Transforming

Perspectives of/on Professional Practice: A Critical Approach

As mentioned earlier, there seems to be a consensus about the humanities and social sciences contributing constructively to practical professional management training. However, there is an angle to this consensus which gives pause for thought. As it happens, we found that few of our interviewees—Mikko Koria from Aalto being the most prominent exception—spoke from personal experience with interdisciplinary professional practice. This means that the respect offered to the social sciences and humanities is largely based on an assumption—a reasonable assumption, to be sure, as these disciplines do teach critical thinking, and Schön's "Reflective Practitioner" (1983) has added significantly to its appreciation in management studies, but an assumption nevertheless, as it has not been tested against reality, at least not as far as we could gauge from our interviews. There are no reliable data available on how much or how little, in what way and to what effect the knowledge taught by the humanities and social sciences impacts on professional management practice, which goes a long way to explain why it is so difficult to sell its practical applicability to students. Coming after what, in the context of our third sub-chapter, sounds like a thoroughly convincing success story, this is an uncomfortable conclusion for the humanities and social sciences—or is it?

Looking at the way in which professional practice is discussed both in our interviews and in published literature on management education, it is evident that these discussions are not or at least not mainly about the humanities' and social sciences' practical applicability but rather about whether academic management education should be about such applicability at all and, if so, in what measure. Opinions as to that, as we showed in our first chapter, are divided between those who argue for more practical applicability and others who claim that the academic approach is a scientific approach which does not and must not try to emulate what professional experience in and of itself can provide much better than any academic teaching could, however practice-oriented, and instead is called upon to prepare students for such experience conceptually, teaching them about the complexity of decision-making rather than telling them what to decide. That this division of opinion is much more pronounced in the published literature than in the material we presented is, of course, due to the fact that the schools we visited have, explicitly or implicitly, already taken their decision about it, coming down clearly on the side of the latter view.

This is not an appeal for academic management education to become even more academic than it already is, ignoring or performatively denigrating the challenges of practical work; indeed, there is no doubt in our eyes that of course management education—like any other type of academic education—must engage with those challenges. But the focus of this engagement also needs some adjusting from an essentialist towards a relational concept of management which renders the boundaries between theory and practice just as permeable as those between disciplines. As Ellen O'Connor has recently pointed out,

> [a] close partnership between academics and practitioners would be ideal. But this would require three radical concessions by academics. They would have to have the same respect for practitioners that they do for academics, they would have to co-create as well as study, and they would have to make the collaboration more important than their disciplines.
>
> *(O'Connor, 2016, p. 46)*

Following the same logic, practitioners on their part would have to respect academics for their contribution to improving professional practice, just as they respect fellow practitioners. They would have to let go of the mixture of awe and disdain that many of them currently display towards academia, they would have to study as well as co-create, and they would have to make the collaboration more important than the notion that all 'real' knowledge about management was taught by practice while viewing the diploma handed out to students at graduation merely as so much documentation that management students were able and willing to suffer for their career goals, instead actively pursuing the enhancement of practice through theory.

This is, of course, easier said than done. From our interviewees' input, we have got the impression that, somewhere between the lines, a certain defensiveness has coloured the various notions of professional practice displayed especially by teaching faculty, as if the whole concept of such practice offered a kind of intrinsic threat to academic management education which had to be either fended off by very broad definitions of it or tamed by underlining that, yes of course, the participation of practitioners in management education was endorsed and even sought after. At the same time, there was little to go on in terms of defining what such practice is or should be from the point of view of business schools and, even more importantly, why there should be such a deep-seated tension between the concept of professional practice and the academic—as opposed to the applicability-oriented or instrumental—approach to it. After all, the humanities and the social sciences educate students towards professional practice just as determinedly as business schools, either within or outside universities, and seeing the increasing scarcity of academic jobs in those fields, most of such practice is conducted outside academia. So what is so special about management education, compared to that which for most other disciplines is simply the reality of the labour market after graduation, certainly different from the life of a student but expectedly and usually more or less productively so, such that 'professional practice' has become such a defining factor for business schools' self-image that it sounds as if it should be spelled with two capital Ps?

The answer to this question possibly lies in the importance which executive education has gained over the years, in terms both of the revenue generated by it and of reputation as recognised by rankings and accreditations. Due to this importance, today there seem to be two groups of primary stakeholders in management education, the one being pre-experience students and the other being the customers of the usually rather expensive post-experience programmes offered by faculty who are accordingly paid high rates for teaching in them. While in our material most faculty teaching undergraduates seem at least moderately optimistic about the effect that transformative teaching, including the humanities and the social sciences, has on the preparation of students for their professional lives after graduation, it was faculty engaging in executive education who were most vocal about the humanities and social sciences having little or nothing to offer to professional practice, implying and sometimes openly stating that these disciplines knew nothing about the two capital Ps and consequently could not relate to it in any way which would significantly enhance paying customers' post-experience educational experience. In the context of executive education, the concept of professional practice, therefore, would seem to be influenced by something of a transference effect. Because selling executive education products is in itself a business and therefore a professional practice, the need to cater to the business practices of its customers' respective professional backgrounds creates a kind of recursive loop—since practitioners of course first and foremost pay for executive education to enhance their grip on their daily business, and since it is the daily business of providers of such education to shape their programmes according to their clients' wishes, professional practice cannot but take on a significance out of all proportion to whatever academic education as such is designed to offer.

For executive education, this is of course legitimate and even necessary, but it may become a problem when faculty teaching both in executive and in undergraduate education carry their concept of professional practice from the former over into the latter, as it then tends to contribute to students' predilection for instrumental learning. We would therefore like to suggest that the concept of practice as communicated by business schools might bear some critical investigation, especially in the interests of students. Students cannot be blamed when they enter business schools expecting to be provided with tool-boxes ready for practical use, as both their previous schooling and the public image of business schools being mainly concerned with instrumental skills prepare them for such expectations long before they set foot into a classroom. Business schools, however, can and must be blamed if they do not at least try to break up the habitual identification of practical with instrumental knowledge which informs such expectations.

To sum up, there is one close tie between students' difficulties with recognising the benefits of transformative management education including the humanities and social sciences, teachers' difficulties with developing transformative teaching modes and the problem of defining the relationship between academic and practical skills, namely all three are based on an understanding of academic knowledge which rests on the belief that such knowledge depicts reality objectively and precisely, that is, they are based on an ontological understanding of knowledge. This is why students seek it in the manner of looking for instruments to deal with the said reality efficiently; this is why teachers are used to feel secure in distributing information *ex cathedra* on what they perceive reality to be; this is why the notion of professional practice as the sphere in which such knowledge is to be used is treated as the touchstone of successful management education, since it is believed to represent the reality of the object studied at business schools in its entirety. As we will show in the following chapter, many of the difficulties in implementing transformative management education as an interdisciplinary endeavour together with the humanities and social sciences derive from this ontological understanding of knowledge, as opposed to the more epistemological understanding of it advocated by the humanities and social sciences.

3

TRANSFORMING KNOWLEDGE

Towards Tomorrow's Needs

Again, the main title of this chapter is deliberately ambiguous, since the material we present here deals with both knowledge about transformation and the transformation of knowledge. As we have shown in our previous chapter, the knowledge necessary to shift management education from the instrumental to the more transformative is not easily accessible to students or teachers, not least because transformative education reaches out both to students' experiential learning outside the classroom and teachers' personal involvement with them, bringing a type of knowledge into play which has not yet become explicitly part of management education. This means that, even before tackling the issue of interdisciplinary knowledge transfer between management studies and the humanities and social sciences, the concept of knowledge informing traditional management education is already being performatively de-balanced.

To talk about knowledge as we do, and especially the concept of knowledge in what we term traditional management education, is of course underpinned by several presuppositions which need explaining. To start with what we describe as 'traditional' management education, we depart from students' expectations of it as being mainly instrumental in nature, presented in our previous chapter. The fact that these expectations are what they are hints at management education having for quite some time displayed and perhaps even advocated this supposition, thus shaping its image for students to latch onto accordingly. Since those expectations, and consequently students' general attitude towards management education, often clash with what transformative management education is trying to achieve for them, we use the term 'traditional' to mark the *status quo* from which the business schools we visited aim to depart.

As to the manner in which we talk about knowledge, our point of departure here is the ontological concept of knowledge as a naturally given entity to be retrieved rather than constructed through research which informed the early Humboldtian university, since our findings suggest that this essentialism still influences the attitude of scholars towards their respective disciplinary domains today. At the same time, the findings suggest that it is mainly this attitude which makes interdisciplinary knowledge transfer so hard to practise, since transformative education demands a much more epistemological approach, especially where increasing students' awareness of the agenda implicit in the content they are taught, through continuously reframing it, is concerned, as this awareness ultimately enables them to recognise that the disciplinary segregation of knowledge is a cultural artefact instead of a description of reality. Consequently, an epistemological approach to knowledge, when challenging disciplinary boundaries, also challenges the concepts of reality defined by those boundaries. What we term 'knowledge', therefore, pertains not to a clearly defined corpus of information, either in management studies or in the humanities and social sciences, but to the ways of relating to reality that are intrinsic to the domains of knowledge encoded by academic disciplines.

That the ways of relating to reality taught by traditional academic management education are perceived to be insufficient to meet the needs of twenty-first-century management was brought up by many of our interviewees. Thomas Lavelle, lecturer in SSE's Department of Law, Languages and Economic Statistics, put it pointedly: "No matter how good we are teaching today's knowledge, it will not be adequate for tomorrow's needs" (interview, 2015). One of the key questions raised by this point—and the question to which this chapter is dedicated—is what the ideal body of knowledge being taught at business schools today should look like, especially in view of the humanities' and social sciences' contribution to it. Investigating this question with our interviewees, we found that, instead of leading towards any kind of definition of content, the question always moved in the direction of the ways and means in which knowledge about management and management education is conceptualised. There were three main threads which ran through the statements we gathered on this issue, according to which we structure our chapter. The first part pertains to the concept of knowledge about management underlying today's management education; the second part deals with what is seen—or expected—to be the contribution of the humanities; the third and final part focuses on how the academic notion of disciplinary education impacts on transformative management education integrating the humanities and social sciences.

"A Successful Catch-all of Nothingness": Concepts of Management

To find out about the concepts of management informing management education in the business schools we visited proved more difficult than we had thought. We had rather naively believed that it would be easy for our interviewees to give us a short but comprehensive run-down about what they saw as the ultimate goal, as well as the pedagogic means of the current and/or emerging management education at their respective institutions, but that proved not to be the case. Perhaps the most pointed comment in this respect came from LUMS Professor Bogdan Costea, who explained that this was not *per se* an educators' problem but rather a problem of global society applying the term 'management' too liberally to narrow it down to any common purpose. This term, Costea explained,

> has been made to stand for so much, it's almost like Weber: once you have a category that seems to explain everything, it tends to explain nothing. It's such an overextended term, it becomes dysfunctional, like 'progress'. It may well describe a certain tendency in a certain area such as post-scale society, but with management it's made to stand for everything and nothing. The thing with this dysfunctionality is that it is successful, it doesn't call for its replacement. [. . .] It's a successful catch-all of nothingness.
>
> *(interview, 2015)*

That this should be so, Costea argued, is due to the fact that the disciplinary segregation of knowledge implemented by Humboldt has, over the last two centuries, allowed those disciplines to drift apart in the name of professional specialisation, to such a point that their common roots are no longer recognisable. For management education, with its rather unspecific disciplinary profile and long history of applicability-oriented teaching, as well as for the humanities and social sciences, in his eyes this means grave losses for both sides:

> What gets lost, also for the humanities, is a connection with a long tradition of thinking about these issues. We lose the classical sources because we lose the ability to read these sources—say Adam Smith. All these key authors get lost. They were humanists, philosophers, economists etc. It is not a museum of ideas. These are the foundational ideas that have shaped how we live together. The European Union (EU) would be impossible without the classical ideas about society, economy, culture, etc. We need to read these classics—Weber, Marx and many others. Can you think about European music without knowing Bach? No, you couldn't. Can you be innovative without [them]? No, you couldn't. The more the world asks us to engage in these questions, the more we discover how poorly equipped we have become to actually respond to this.
>
> *(interview, 2015)*

The statement "it is not a museum of ideas" at first glance refers to the types of knowledge managed by the humanities, reflecting the clichéd impression that the humanities have become too disconnected from reality to contribute meaningfully to management education. At second glance, however, the 'it' in this sentence includes the academic domains of both the humanities and management education, implying that the latter have grown just as inflexible and hegemonic in distributing pre-set disciplinary packages of knowledge as the former, thus turning students' educational experience at a business school into a more or less guided walk through a collection of old and quite possibly rather musty-smelling artefacts.

Throughout our interviews, such calls for increasing the vitality of the knowledge imparted by management educators has been a constant in our interviewees' concerns, echoing strongly the complaints made by authors from Khurana (2007) to Thomas et al. (2014) about the decline of said relevance. More often than not, we were informed that the basic education in management consisted of what was sometimes, in the time-honoured formula, referred to as "the usual suspects", implying that there was an established body of knowledge which constituted the know-how presumed to be essential to management students. "The first two years", we were told by Joan Rodón Mòdol at ESADE, "are composed by a generalist education comprising courses in math, stats, accounting, sociology, organisation, law, econ, IT and operations" (interview, 2015). Looking at the curricula offered by the business schools we visited, this seems to be—with minor deviations—a generally agreed-on standard, conformed to more or less as a matter of course by both students and educators, and referred to by Jan Molin, dean of education at CBS, as "the pure management disciplines" (interview, 2014).

While the questions we asked thus yielded very little positive characterisation of what those "pure management disciplines" are about, in terms of their content, the critical assessments of their present shape allow us to infer a kind of characterisation *ex negativo*. At CBS, for instance, Kristian Kreiner, director of the Centre for Management Studies of the Building Process, stated that the way in which CBS tries to go about management education

> is not about developing knowledge for practice. We teach them why it is difficult to teach management, why [it] is problematic to make decisions. The act of being a manager is the act of making accounts, making a strategy. The purpose is to understand why [it] is so difficult to make good strategy. In the books [it] is easy to make a good strategy . . . but reality is not so.
>
> *(interview, 2014)*

Likewise, as mentioned in the previous chapter, Sven Bislev, vice-dean of education at CBS, stressed the need to build up the awareness of the dependence of management decisions on the individual backgrounds or, as he phrased it, the "subjectivity of the students":

> This complicated universe of ideas and actions is one way in which students' subjectivity encounters a large universe of meanings. [. . .] From an automated model—because you are rational, action always follows from your knowledge—to a much more nuanced and complicated view, where

action is a choice that is made on the basis not only of your knowledge, but of the context and your maturity. We are human, not machines, cogs in a wheel. Subjectivity is where we do 'our things'.

(interview, 2014)

At SSE, Thomas Lavelle was similarly certain that for future managers "to have technical knowledge is not enough" and that the current "business school approach to learning in an instrumental manner" needed to be improved on because "our students must be prepared for an uncertain future and this is not covered by our current ways and models of teaching marketing, finance, etc." Therefore, he argued stringently for a "meta-discourse to explain what management education should be about, in order to change the expectations of our students", admitting that, "[r]ather than challenging their epistemological frameworks, we are currently satisfying them and therefore inhibiting their development" (interview, 2015).

According to Theodore Vurdubakis, head of the Department of Organisation, Work and Technology at LUMS, in students' expectations of management education "the longing for management becomes the longing for the impossible object. You want a tool to solve the problem before you know what the problem is. The technique they want to learn does not exist" (interview, 2015). Following up on that, Lucas Introna, professor in the same department, elaborated,

> One problem that management has made was to make management into a normative science, so the idea that there is a way you ought to be, you ought to be rational, you ought to take decisions, so it's this normatisation vis-à-vis the daily existential experience of being a manager, of being in an organisation. And when the question comes up, "What is management?", you ask the people in the organisation, what do they do? And they will tell you things like "we talk, we discuss, we agree, we decide, we do these things". There's nothing fantastical about this, it's not magical. What makes management seem different is the normative, the way that we cut this in order to produce something that is now strategic, operational, has an object, has visions. We've constructed this object which is management, and somehow, we want people to believe in that because, of course, this legitimises the institutions. [. . .] From the point of the academic world, we have to define management in a particular way, and we have to defend its boundaries. Of course, there are some technical domains like accounting, but beyond the technical domain there's ordinary everyday life and it's difficult really to know in that domain. It's practical wisdom you require, it's not a theory. [. . .] Unfortunately, the management and business schools are in this process of continuously legitimating management as something exceptional, different to other things because this is what we sell, this is why

we have all these people at our door because they think this is something exceptional, something we give them, a box of tools, answers, and this is what they want.

(interview, 2015)

In the eyes of both students and management educators, the content of management education has crystallised into a mainly technical domain. The concept of knowledge about management education underlying the production of such content implies that the perfect manager functions strictly rationally and, moreover, that the rationality in question can be both clearly defined and clearly taught, as well as being transferable into any given context of professional practice. This in turn provokes students' expectation that, during their time at university, they are going to be provided with a set of skills that will be ready for application.

The body of knowledge traditionally taught at business schools thus seems to suffer from a malaise induced by two components that are inextricably intermeshed with each other. One component is this body's technical orientation, a problem which is one of how management and management education are perceived and indeed used by the relevant stakeholder groups from students via educators up to and including the societal context of management. The very practical applicability of management education, at least for students, significantly reduces the costs of opportunity in their choice of career, as they see management methodology less as an object of scientific curiosity and more as a commodity to be acquired for future use which, through the growing emphasis placed on business and the economy by society as a whole, promises an almost certain success in their professional lives. The other component is an academic system which, by defining management as a scientific object, has made management education into a rather curious hybrid. While the practical applicability of the knowledge dispensed is management education's goal, and as such, its unique selling point (especially compared to other academic disciplines like, for example, the humanities and social sciences, whose content is rather less evidently applicable), the historically grown logic of disciplinary segregation inherent in the academic system seems to have deprived this knowledge of the flexibility necessary to adapt to the ever-changing challenges of its professional practice, in a world which evolves far faster than the methodological needs to which universities are systemically equipped to cater.

Emerging from these and multiple other, if less pointed statements made in much the same vein is an image of the ideal management education which differs from its current shape in three important points. Firstly, at least for management educators, the image of the *homo oeconomicus* dating back to nineteenth-century business practice and normalised by business schools not much later, in the course of their being integrated into universities and related institutional structures, has run the course of its usefulness, as it no longer complies with the characteristics and capabilities needed by managers in the twenty-first century. Secondly, as much of the current problems of management education are attributed to the pressure that the academic system exerts on the content of what is being taught, reforming management education effectively depends on reforming either the academic system as a whole or at least redefining management's relationship with it so as to create an educational space which allows for teaching about the specific societal contexts and relevance of management practices. Thirdly, and intrinsically connected to the former point, for any management education of the future, it is believed that, instead of receiving a pre-set body of knowledge, students should be taught critically to reflect on the framework or frameworks of the knowledge they are receiving. Through this, they should be made to realise that, however seemingly objective the content offered to them might appear, this content is in fact generated by and thus transporting contextually situated values and standards. As Professor Josep Lozano from ESADE concisely summed it up: "We need to reframe their understanding of management, if not we cannot teach differently" (interview, 2015).

The Something-Factor: What the Humanities (Are Supposed to) Know About Management and Business

Our questions as to why the schools we visited were turning to the humanities and social sciences to improve management education, and what they either knew or hoped their contribution would be elicited a broad variety of experiences, expectations and beliefs in response. Before our interviews, we had assumed that the direction these statements took would depend on whether there was—or was about to be—a part of the curriculum dedicated to the teaching of humanities and social sciences at the respective school, or whether they were introduced by management educators as part of their course content without such explicit institutional endorsement. It turned out that we were wrong in this assumption, as interviewees at some of the schools who work on the basis of implicit approval were much more specific in giving voice to their notion of the humanities than others who taught in frameworks which explicitly endorse their integration. Overall, however, it quickly became clear that there is indeed a specific set of skills or competences attributed to the humanities, even if their operational value for and status in management education often remains rather vague.

One of the topics most regularly linked to the humanities by our interviewees was interpretative skills. "You do need the humanities", Sue Cox, then-dean of LUMS, asserted.

We have so much data today, but how to interpret it? It comes back to reflexivity as a capability. In problem-solving, interpretation is absolutely essential. [. . .] There is so much data generation in finance and marketing, but who teaches us how to structure, interpret and present this?

(interview, 2015)

For Emma Stenström, associate professor in the Department of Management and Organisation at SSE, "interpretations" are what the humanities are best at and provide knowledge about (interview, 2015), and for Vincent Kaufmann, who chaired the Contextual Studies programme at HSG for more than ten years, interpretation is equally crucial: "Interpretation competence is very important. The core of the humanities is hermeneutics and interpretation. This is the core competence we can provide to business students" (interview, 2015).

As to what interpretation is, how it can be taught and where it takes place, however, opinions differ. In the catalogue of knowledge areas that the task force charged with developing a strategy for the reform of Koç University's core curriculum drew up, "Aesthetics and Interpretive Understanding" is listed first, interestingly being followed directly by the humanities and the social sciences, which thus are set apart from it. For "Aesthetics and Interpretive Understanding", the strategy paper explains,

> Courses offered under this category will familiarize students with the cultural fabric of Turkey and the world, introduce students to a number of artistic and literary traditions, and help them understand and appreciate the thoughts, feelings, and beliefs expressed in a variety of artistic and literary fields in an informed and critical way. It is essential for these courses to expose students to critical assessment, aesthetic criteria, and to develop ability for interpretive understanding; express the significance of different artistic and literary forms as a reflection of human intellect, heart, and soul; emphasize the meaning and value of appreciating diverse approaches.
>
> *(see https://core.ku.edu.tr/about-the-core-program/)*

For "The Humanities", the paper says,

> Humanities cover a broad range of topics including history, philosophy, law, and to some extent arts and literature where major aspects of humanity are discussed. It is crucial to build an intellectual foundation for inquiry, to understand the factors shaping the thought, culture, belief, and society and to recognize the interplay between them in an informed and critical way.
>
> *(see https://core.ku.edu.tr/portfolio-item/hums/)*

While at first glance the difference between the explanations of the two may seem negligible, it is the adjective 'intellectual' which marks out the rift between the different knowledge areas as perceived by the task force. In their eyes, the humanities are more concerned with rigorously intellectual processes than with direct exposure to aesthetic experiences, the latter being much encouraged at SSE and CBS as well. This also perhaps explains why Aalto University's School of Business never raised the question of whether to engage with the humanities during the university's recent fundamental reorganisation, instead supporting the university governors' decision to engage with art and design.

Closely linked to the 'intellectual' image of the humanities is the perception that they, more than other disciplines, teach critical thinking. For Caspar Hirschi, professor of history at HSG and currently co-chair of the contextual studies reform process, this is one of the central contributions of the humanities:

> I think that one common ground would be to speak about critical thinking. The tradition of criticism, critical analysis of structures, etc. is really firmly rooted in humanities, including philology and philosophy. Of course, there are critical economists as well, for example, but here expertise in economics *per se* is more important than critical thinking competences.
>
> *(interview, 2015)*

Martin Eppler, professor of media studies at HSG, who holds a doctorate in Linguistics, Semiotics and Organisational science, argues similarly:

> For me it is very clear what is the contribution of humanities. In a functional dimension, [it is] a better grasp on management problems or relevant topics, to be more creative, or to understand the phenomena better with the help of humanities. Humanities is a tool for creativity, for understanding, for reflection. The normative dimension not only tells you how to reach certain goals but also tells you which goals are worth attaining.
>
> *(interview, 2015)*

Professor James Tang, dean of the School of Social Sciences at SMU and chair of the task force "humanities@smu" charged with developing a strategy for the integration of the humanities and social sciences, elaborated further on why this particular ability is important to him:

> [T]hinking more critically, asking [a] different kind of questions, develop[ing a] different kind of perspectives—this sort of skills is increasingly in demand, regardless of whether you are an economist, accountant, senior manager. I suppose social sciences broadly teach students to understand problems, not just particular sets of solutions, but also what a solution *means*. When you have a problem, there are different ways of tackling the problem, and different ways have different consequences and parities.
>
> *(interview, 2014)*

"Reflecting more than what we can calculate" through seeing "the traditional management disciplines in a context" is, for Professor Jan Molin, dean of education at CBS, one of the main learning goals in integrating the humanities:

> The game we are trying to orchestrate is epistemological. We try to convey that different disciplines have different methods and approaches and that what is required is to understand those models of reality and their assumptions and allow students to understand how to be flexible in applying them.
>
> *(interview, 2014)*

Critical thinking is, then, compounded of several elements: the ability to deal with volatility, uncertainty, complexity and ambiguity as encoded in the Harvard VUCA-paradigm strongly emphasised by Martin Eppler; the ability to recognise, choose from and if necessary adapt different methodologies to different problems instead of blindly sticking to a pre-formed recipe and also both the will and the ability to engage with societal values on a moral level.

This latter component was touched on by nearly every business school that we visited, usually under the concept of ethics. At Koç, Ethical Reasoning is one of the knowledge areas to be included in the reformed core programme; at Aalto, business ethics is part of the curriculum as a matter of course, and at SSE, the "importance of ethics" was affirmed in a group interview with Anthony Magistrale, Ken Wagner and Thomas Lavelle: "We need to pay attention to philosophers, literary critics. This is part of the humanities" (interview, 2015). At HSG, Martin Eppler stated that "to have ethical ambitions, not purely financial[ly] driven ambitions" was part of the university's vision for its students (interview, 2015); at SMU, ethics was seen as being part of its foundational claim to educate responsible leaders, the teaching practice of which, for James Tang, could be improved by "a stronger problem-orientation, taking up issues" (interview, 2014), and at ESADE, the teaching of ethics is rooted in the concept of *iustitia*, one of the four pillars of the Jesuit educational tradition, and thus equally deeply embedded in the school's foundational impetus.

While ethics thus seems to have gained an unequivocal standing in management education (so much so that, at Aalto, we raised eyebrows by even asking about it), its impact on the perception of the humanities and their role in management education was viewed rather critically by some of our interviewees at LUMS. In many of the reports on management education which have been written since the recent financial crises, ethics was cited as the most important contribution made by the humanities. This has coloured the view of the humanities so deeply that, in some reports, and most explicitly in the recent Carnegie report (Colby et al., 2011), the humanities are mainly expected to help students improve morally, to become better human beings. Laurence Hemming, professor in the

Department of Politics, Philosophy and Religion at LUMS, criticised this view as inadequate:

> It is the presupposition of the Carnegie report that a liberal education, or liberal arts education will prepare you for a good life. [. . .] You would be laughed out of court if you raised that as a way for the humanities to proceed. It's almost precisely that understanding of education that is dissolved by the humanities.
>
> *(interview, 2015)*

Bogdan Costea, in the same interview, elaborated further that, in his eyes,

> the Carnegie report fails to understand business education completely. From one end to another they did not get the fact that business schools (a) do not lack [. . .] humanism, they have the most powerful humanism and they have been playing with the humanities for forty years: theatre, drama, literature, poetry, narrative, storytelling, music, performativity—every performance art, consultancy and management education have been doing it! [. . .] And (b) what they failed to realise is: even if they [the humanities] got the licence and someone said to them "please come in and save us", they would perforate this over-humanising demand, that's *hubris*, that the humanities would make them a proper human being. [. . .] It's not about humanisation.
>
> *(interview, 2015)*

For Costea, this heritage meant that it is not the morally normative but the reflective component of critical thinking which needs to be conveyed to students: "I'm not telling them *how* to think, but how to raise the question. [. . .] It's not a question of giving them an answer but to open up the question" (interview, 2015). This certainly does not mean that he avoided talking about values; in his eyes, the role of the humanities was not to provide orientational knowledge in the sense of defining a clear framework of ethics within which to practise management, but rather to have the students question how values are created as such, to hone their awareness of values' situatedness, the fact that they are not given absolutely but constructed under conditions which determine their content and direction. From this perspective, Costea strongly disagreed with the point of departure that most current debates on management education choose to argue for reforming it, i.e. that the global economy is in a crisis to which management education has to react by improving the personalities of its students; instead, he claimed, "The real crisis is in our *understanding* of where value comes from", and it is this understanding which should be improved through the humanities (interview, 2015). Similarly, Thomas Lavelle at SSE specified that his understanding of critical thinking was definitively not that of a moralistic attitude, as "a critical approach to business does not have to be understood in a negative manner, nor be understood as disruptive, on the contrary. It creates a type of check", a kind of intellectual touchstone validating solutions to problems instead of judging them (interview, 2015).

Besides interpretational abilities, critical thinking and the engagement with moral values, a fourth competence was seen as a unique selling point of the humanities, already hinted at in the Koç task force paper and in the comments of Bogdan Costea, namely the providing of historical context to techniques used and problems encountered in the practice of management. In Costea's words,

> If there's anything that schools could do, it's to return to scholarship, it has nothing to do with the formation of the creature, it has to do with the cultivation of a way of preserving the manifestation of the human spirit, it's a kind of a preservation of heritage.
>
> *(interview, 2015)*

More concretely, Ulrich Schmid, professor of Russian at the HSG School of Humanities and Social Sciences (SHSS), told us,

> What I try to do when I explain the *raison d'être* of why I am here, I emphasise my contribution as giving the historical and cultural background for economic, legal and managerial processes. This might be a big claim but this is what I try to do.
>
> *(interview, 2015)*

Through this, Schmid aims at supplying students with knowledge which they are not taught in their core courses:

> Most management professors like to boil things down to a model—take the St. Gallen management model (Rüegg-Stürm & Grand, 2015) as a case in point. It is a sophisticated scheme, and we humanities scholars tend to shy away from constructing such schemes because it reduces certain phenomena and models tend to ignore historical background. You have the concept of path-dependency but I don't think this really takes issue with historical and cultural background. It remains blind to inertia.
>
> *(interview, 2015)*

Thomas Beschorner, HSG professor of business ethics (also part of the SHSS), described the contribution of the humanities as follows:

> To reflect about the role of business in society, how are they embedded in [a] concrete societal context; to widen the understanding of what organisations are, beyond this financial-reductionist economic rationality understanding from management and economics. A more holistic, interpretative

approach, to inform and discuss with students that in organisations there are many language games going on at the same time (politics, bureaucracy, values), to provide students with a much richer, broader and complex understanding of how businesses function; also, to discuss normative issues, the normative role of ethics and morality.

(interview, 2015)

From outside the SHSS came similar comments by James Davis, dean of the School of Economics and Political Science at HSG: "So students don't know the history of the debates which have shaped our disciplines. We privilege method over substance and historical context" (interview, 2015). Furthermore, according to Kuno Schedler, professor of public management and then-dean of the School of Management:

> Here in St. Gallen the main contribution [of the humanities] is to broaden the perspectives of our students. If we only focus on functionalities in management we do have a problem. From the perspective of [the School of Management], if you are too narrow, you breed a certain type of future manager that does not have the wide perspective that he needs to succeed as a manager in a complex environment. History, philosophy, sociology, all these topics are part of a broader perspective of management.
>
> *(interview, 2015)*

All in all, interpretation (including media competence), critical thinking, morality and historical competence were seen to be the four most important constituents of the claim by the humanities and social sciences to make a contribution to management education. A number of other topics also repeatedly emerged, most prominent among them the promotion of communication and media competences and the fostering of creativity through aesthetic experience. These latter topics, though, like the self-evidential existence of ethics in present-day business school curricula, were mostly treated as a matter of course, without meriting the succinct and sometimes rather heated statements that we received on the former, indicating that the former are at the core of what management education is currently lacking and expects the humanities and social sciences to provide.

While there is thus a general consensus on the content of what the humanities and social sciences should provide, there were, however, some serious doubts repeatedly expressed about whether and how they could and/or are prepared to do so practically. At SSE, Thomas Lavelle stated that "the humanities need to change their audience, not only writing for humanities scholars" (interview, 2015). He went on to explain that the intra-disciplinary type of discourse favoured by such scholars is currently still much too opaque and hermetic to be able to convey the kind of knowledge sought after by management education. Thus, this discourse fosters resentment towards it by creating the impression that humanities scholars claim hegemonic privileges in construing reality: "There is richness in the multiplicity of the approaches. The humanities do not have a monopoly in all the valuable ways of expressing, other approaches are also valuable" (interview, 2015). Therefore, these disciplines need to shape up to be able to communicate the content of their contribution to knowledge about management in a way to which management students can relate: "The intrinsic value of what is being offered should be displayed, this is very important in a business school, because humanities scholars are there to offer their value, they need to translate their knowledge and values" (interview, 2015). A similar assessment was offered by James Tang at SMU, who, in terms of educational credibility, distinguished between the humanities and the social sciences:

> Social science tends to be more explicit about its own methods and ways of approaching problems and what it can contribute. Humanities tend to be less explicit in general about how they can be brought to bear on solving problems. Humanities professors tend to take for granted that the contributions they make are self-evident.
>
> *(interview, 2014)*

At ESADE, when questioned about the use of the humanities and social sciences, Professor Daniel Arenas Vives, chair of the Department of Social Sciences, told us that he would not want "to be the one counting the impact of the humanities" in the way the impact of management studies was measured, because for him, the humanities were not designed to create impact: "Humanities do not have to have a purpose; if you want that, then don't call it 'Humanities', or specify [. . .] 'Humanities in Business Education'" (interview, 2015)

Even where, as at HSG, the contribution of the humanities and social sciences amounts to a quarter of the credit points to be achieved by every student, through contextual studies, the notion of their constitutional purposelessness clings tenaciously to their image—and not, as Simon Evenett, professor of economics at HSG with a strong focus on decision-making, explained, because of their content as such, but because of a perceived lack of willingness on the part of humanities and social sciences scholars to engage actively in the concerns of management education:

> Nothing of what I say would imply a constraint of the possible contributions of humanities and social sciences to business education. There is no inherent constraint. The importance of context is well established, there are important aspects of corporate strategy that deal with it. So, there are whole areas of business that could be informed by the social sciences and the humanities. But what I do not see is people in those fields prepared to do the work. [. . .] Professors need to want to do this transformation. For some it is even a point of pride to be totally uninterested about what is happening in the world. This is unhelpful.
>
> *(interview, 2015)*

Even more outspoken is the criticism raised by Bogdan Costea at LUMS against the disciplines of the humanities and social sciences and the scholars representing them, set against the background of his belief that doing business was and is at the centre of any given cultural development and thus should be a crucial issue for these scholars:

> They are a catastrophe. They have become divorced from the traditions that created them. They no longer help us to understand contemporary problems of value, what value is and might be today. They have become detached from their own origins, and therefore from the engagement with questions about contemporary value crises. They are not delivering interesting questions. The humanities and social sciences are in a crisis of their own. [. . .] The social sciences and humanities would benefit from re-entering in a very substantive—and it would have to be a substantive— dialogue about how management and business is a core cultural, social, economic, political, diplomatic, legal domain of common inquiry. It is not a question of one fixing the other or one being more scientific than the other. All these games in academia are useless.
>
> *(interview, 2015)*

Part of the problem is an issue which is put most clearly by Costea but pervades many other interviews as well: the question of what precisely distinguishes the humanities from management studies if, as those convinced that integrating the former into the latter is the way to go for business schools, they supply crucial competences to future managers. For Costea, management studies and the humanities are close, if not identical in terms of content, but have drifted apart under the pressure of disciplinary specialisation. By Seppo Ikäheimo, professor of finance and accounting at Aalto University School of Business, we were told that he saw no need whatsoever to integrate the humanities into management education because "management education is 100% humanities, because everything we do deals with human behaviour" (interview, 2015). Similarly, Josep Lozano at ESADE said that "we should understand humanities as everything related to human beings and human development; if not, management is not related to human beings" (interview, 2015). From the point of view of management teachers, these statements contest a certain *hubris* perceived to be connected with the term 'humanities', implying that one of the impediments to integrating them might well be their—assumed or factual—presumption in claiming exclusive knowledge about what really matters to human beings as opposed to, for instance, management studies.

Summing up, there appears to be a significant gap between perceptions as to what and how the humanities and social sciences could contribute to management education, on the one hand, and perceptions as to what, in fact, they are willing or equipped to offer, on the other. While there is a consensus that the four types of knowledge outlined earlier belong to their domain of disciplinary knowledge and thus constitute their unique selling points for management education requirements, at the same time, there are deep misgivings as to their practical abilities to deliver the goods, partly because of the historically grown image of the humanities as a purely intellectual endeavour, partly because of the inability of its disciplinary representatives to translate their content into a language which can be understood by both management students and management education's societal stakeholders.

Discipline Matters: Concepts of Integrated Knowledge

"It is not a joke", Vincent Kaufmann at HSG assured us when he told us about having delivered a lecture entitled "Fuck the Disciplines" some years ago (interview, 2015). For him, as for many others of our interviewees across the schools that we visited, the assignment of types of knowledge to disciplinary domains under the framework of the Humboldtian university system is a fundamental problem of present-day academic education. As such, this problem is seen to be responsible for most of the difficulties in reforming management education through the integration of the humanities and social sciences.

How schools which engage in interdisciplinary management education deal with these challenges is mainly influenced by the status of the school's official endorsement of the integration of the humanities. Overall, we found both explicit and implicit institutional endorsements, which appear in two sub-types, respectively. Explicit endorsement of integration can either work on the principle of add-on knowledge, meaning that part of management students' curricula is officially dedicated to courses instructing them in the knowledge imparted by the humanities, whether or not such knowledge is actively shaped towards the needs of management students, or it can work on the principle that humanities knowledge definitely needs to be encoded towards management education, thus encouraging, for example, team teaching and research by humanities and management scholars in dedicated parts of the curricula. Integration taking place under implicit institutional endorsement, on the other hand, can either mean that teachers are encouraged to integrate whatever types of knowledge they think appropriate to the subject they teach into their courses, or that management is seen to be about humanity anyway, so that, in fact, keeping up with the humanities is considered to be a precondition of management studies and vice versa.

Among the schools we visited, SSE is the one with, on the surface, the least explicit institutional endorsement of including the humanities. "It is not the classical American model of what are the humanities, but our way with humanities. This puts demand on teachers. They need to know these things", explained Jesper Blomberg, associate professor of management at SSE (interview, 2015). According to Blomberg, "The thread is that we should embrace knowledge from different disciplines", which rests very much with the teachers themselves: "Integration is not encouraged at the teaching level. It is all done because of personal interests". While other departments remain focused on their disciplinary domains, he added, the Department of Management and Organisation actively pursues interdisciplinary integration:

> The management department is the place where this discussion about the humanities is taking place, in comparison with finance, accounting . . . We are protecting this wider view of knowledge that we should be giving to our students. This is stereotyping, because the professors in accounting, they are interested in these topics as well, but this does not have an impact on the course material, whereas in the management department's case it really makes a difference.
>
> *(interview, 2015)*

In the SSE Department of Law, Languages and Economic Statistics, Thomas Lavelle was rather more sceptical about the potential for integration, the main problem with it being, in his view, that the domains of knowledge in the different disciplines are more or less inaccessible to scholars from other disciplines: "The language of accounting means one cannot access knowledge as it is needed but needs to learn first the language of accounting" (interview, 2015). Therefore, he believed that, "because languages are so different, the best we can hope for is a pseudo-interdisciplinarity". To change that,

> we would need to revisit the accessibility of today's disciplinary knowledge. The forms in which [it is] expressed are resistant. The only way to access the accounting knowledge is to go through the ladder of the discipline. It is not meant to be accessed quickly and rapidly.
>
> *(interview, 2015)*

From the point of view of students, on the other hand, the interdisciplinary teaching practices of the Department of Management are valued. Isak, who took a bachelor's degree in architecture and is currently studying banking and finance, told us that

> all the subjects studied at SSE are presented under the scientific logic and this means that the rational approach predominates. [. . .] These skills are very valuable for business, the danger is in forgetting that we are autonomous units, we are part of a culture and this is why I think it is so important we permeate business studies with culture. [. . .] We do not learn to be creative, we are just getting prescriptive models (very good in telling us 'how to build') but not inquiring into the whys, which type of society do we want, how can we imagine our society?
>
> *(interview, 2015)*

What Isak appreciated most was the encouragement that students receive to engage with modern art, of which SSE holds a collection. Isak is one of the co-founders of the student associations' Art Initiative, which not long ago created a small but notable scandal by installing a video in the entrance hall of SSE showing a naked man dancing. Around this, the students organised a number of talks and discussions:

> The idea is to support these ideas with art talks. It is not enough to bring the art to the school, but we need to create a discursive platform to enhance the knowledge about art and therefore allow for meaningful discussions. These discussions are interdisciplinary, art, economics, etc.
>
> *(interview, 2015)*

The institution not only allows but actively enables these activities, seeing the engagement with art as an important channel for exposing students to the complexities of the humanities' knowledge domains. Emma Stenström told us that the implicit endorsement of the humanities as practised by SSE is based on encouraging interventional intent both in curricular and in extracurricular activities of the students: "Art brings other things, embodiment, the senses, making sense with the senses" (interview, 2015). Merely teaching, for example, art history, on the other hand, reinforces what she referred to as today's "formalised relationship with art".

Both CBS and LUMS work with explicit institutional endorsement for including the humanities on a programme-based level. CBS has been running several interdisciplinary programmes for years, mainly from the Department of Management and Philosophy. Sine Just, one of the directors of the programme Sociology and Management, told us that in her programme they tried to avoid having 'parallel disciplines' teaching "economic sociology, where we try to mix in one course the disciplines [. . .] by a combination of courses in each discipline with a single exam", an endeavour which still met with some resistance even among faculty: "There is an argument that if we are teaching the basics, then we should test disciplinary knowledge before we do the integration" (interview, 2014). When asked about how and where the different types of knowledge were aligned with each other in the programme, Edward Ashbee, also one of its directors, explained that this mainly depended on the students themselves, as the teachers were impeded by their disciplinary backgrounds:

> It is difficult [for] someone that is an expert in economic history to make connections with business studies, same the other way around. All the disciplines are narrowly defined, and we are urging the students to make the connections. [. . .] The hope is that after three years they will be able to integrate the different knowledges by themselves.
>
> *(interview, 2014)*

At LUMS, Bogdan Costea was deeply sceptical about sustainably establishing interdisciplinarity within the present academic system. While the then-dean of LUMS, Sue Cox, actively supported integrating the humanities, and Costea himself practised this integration passionately, he doubted that it would be possible to overcome either institutional restrictions or the ingrained disciplinary self-concept of scholars, or at least to moderate them sufficiently for management education with integrated humanities components to become anything like a mainstream phenomenon. LUMS runs two groups or types of programme at the undergraduate level, one group consisting of relatively focused programmes (in accounting, logistics, finance, etc.) and the other consisting of more broadly scoped, interdisciplinary programmes which are organised across the different departments of LUMS. At the time of our visit, LUMS was in the process of establishing a new Bachelor of Science in management, politics and international relations with the explicit goal of nurturing interdisciplinary education and co-operation, as Cox told us,

> Certainly, it is interdisciplinary, it will build on a variety of learning styles, and it will actually make students do what I want them to do, which is to think within domains and across domains. It is easy for us to sit here and say, "We want our students to be critical and reflexive, we want them to be this and that", but you have to have a vehicle for doing that. You're not going to have an 18-year-old who has gone through a fairly rigorous study to think across boundaries without giving them enough appreciation of the underpinning disciplines, and I think that's why these schemes will do that, and I think that the students who will go through this programme will be students that reflect well what we want to do here at Lancaster.
>
> *(interview, 2015)*

While these activities are wholeheartedly embraced by the dean, and the introduction of such new programmes is being supported broadly at the management school (among the 'discursive' as well as 'calculative' disciplines, as Costea put it [interview, 2015]), there is, however, no general reform agenda for all management education programmes at LUMS. "Besides adding programmes, there is no room for integrating humanities", Costea stated, going on to explain that the reason for the fact that faculty is not resistant towards and even accepting of such new programmes might very well be that they were not seriously affected by them, as would be the case if management education as a whole were subjected to a corresponding reform:

> Now, in order to overcome that sort of one-sided view of what is a management school [. . .] and what should humanities *do*, [. . .] that needs an overhaul of a mode of thinking which no programme, not even this little scheme can do. You *cannot* really overcome that mode of orientation [. . .]

by decree, you cannot dis-establish it. [. . .] And how to do it otherwise? What would you do without sounding too dictatorial? [. . .] Personally, I think I will never live to see the day when a discussion like the one we have now would take place as a legitimate concern in an interdisciplinary dialogue. Just the form of it: how would we begin to talk with each other again? I don't think we have the elements of the language to even begin that dialogue.

(interview, 2015)

In terms of institutional endorsement for integrating the humanities, ESADE is a rather special case. Their concept of knowledge(s) to be imparted to management students is firmly based on the set of values defined by the *Societas Jesu* who founded the school in 1958. A position paper, *Educating Managers for the Twenty-first Century*, by Eduard Bonet Guinó, emeritus professor of mathematics at ESADE, describes what this means for management education as follows:

ESADE has updated the Jesus Society's tradition, which is considered a humanistic form of liberal education, and has adapted it to the studies of management: *utilitas* focusses on professional aspects, *justitia* on social responsibility, *humanitas* on humanistic personal development, and *fides* is extended to spirituality.

(Bonet, 2015, p. 13)

While this set of values is binding for all members of the faculty, the ground rules laid down at the foundation of ESADE leave it open as to whether these values are taught in dedicated humanities courses or whether they are to be included in the content of management courses. This, we were told, led to a certain negligence with regard to the focus on these values in teaching, since, under the pressure of accreditations, rankings and publishing conventions, faculty members were found to be concentrating more and more on disciplinary *utilitas* (interview, 2015). Therefore, in 2013, a task force charged with developing suggestions for the improvement of ESADE's flagship programme, the bachelor in business administration (BBA), came to the conclusion that, according to Jesuit tradition,

the dissemination of practical knowledge (*utilitas*) should not be separated from either the integral formation of the individual (*humanitas*), or the preferential treatment of the most vulnerable (*iustitia*), or spiritual formation (*fides*).

(ESADE, 2013, p. 10)

This conclusion implies, as indeed is explained in more detail later in the paper, that the three virtues other than *utilitas* were not being sufficiently supported in the programme's current curriculum, while disciplinarily instrumental knowledge was being over-emphasised. The working paper provides a brief assessment of the status of the four virtues within the existing programme and identifies a number of developmental needs in order better to align the programme with them, with programmatic emphasis placed on *iustitia*, or social justice:

> The basic idea is for the reinforcement of the liberal arts in the BBA [. . .] to be based on the Jesuit Society's traditional teaching model and to strengthen ESADE's teaching model [. . .]. All this must facilitate the incorporation of moral values as an integral part of all subjects and the program as a whole, thereby facilitating the education of participants in a profession in which not only technical skills are important but also the shaping of their moral character.
>
> *(ESADE, 2013, p. 4)*

The reformed BBA, the working paper states, is planned to offer elective courses in the fields of the humanities and social sciences, including literature, history, anthropology, history of religion and philosophy, three of which the students have to choose during their bachelor studies. However, as Joan Rodón Mòdol, programme director of the BBA, explained to us, the idea is not only to add more content and types of knowledge to the curriculum but also to inspire the faculty teaching management to follow suit in the mandatory courses:

> The four virtues provide a basis for the ESADE educational culture, and it must be strengthened in the coming years—both in terms of changing content, adding new humanities courses, but also in terms of having management course professors integrate these virtues in how they teach marketing, accounting, etc.
>
> *(interview, 2015)*

All three of the remaining schools—that is, Koç, HSG and SMU—embrace the principle of integrated education for the whole institution, dedicating part of all curricula as a vessel for teaching types of knowledge that are not covered by the regular majors. Koç University runs what it calls the "core program" where, among other subjects, including the natural sciences, humanities and social sciences, are taught. In 2010, the programme was reformed in order to offer students more flexibility in their choice of courses. Before, there had been eight mandatory courses, which were now replaced by the 'knowledge areas' already mentioned, offering courses on various subjects from which the students can select according to their individual interests. In their working paper on the reform, the task force charged with developing it outlined its goal as follows:

> A well-designed and well-taught core curriculum *inspires collaboration across specializations* by showing students that, no matter how different they are, different disciplines intersect in their concern for common issues that have

to do with individuals, societies, the world, and the universe. [. . .] The era in which we live and which awaits our students does not only require excellence in professional areas but also a sophisticated understanding of the complex nature of the twenty-first century and the integrated nature of the issues in the contemporary world. [. . .] While the core curriculum fulfils students' desire to pursue their learning interest unencumbered with the limitation of high school education or the requirements of professional and vocational identities, it also makes learning relevant for social issues and community problems. Therefore, *the core serves as a bridge between the university and society.*

(see https://core.ku.edu.tr/about-the-core-program/)

For actively linking the content of the courses in the core programme to the content taught in those of the students' majors, however, students and teachers are mostly left to their own devices. Professor Zeynep Gürhan Canlı, associate dean for graduate business programmes, among them the CEMS MIM master programme which is renowned and highly ranked for its interdisciplinary approach to management education, told us that although the "university provides a fruitful context for exploring connections between business and culture in a broad sense", realising those connections in research "is entirely up to the individual researcher", just as it is to the teacher: "I use my intuition and personal experiences" (interview, 2014). Professor Ali Çarkoğlu, dean of undergraduate education, remarked in the same interview that, for integrating different kinds of knowledge, "co-teaching can be helpful. It makes you as a teacher more humble with respect to formulating and solving problems", but again he underlined that it was left up to teachers to decide whether or not to engage with it: "We can't force this upon faculty" (interview, 2014).

At HSG, the teaching of extra-disciplinary subjects has been part of the foundational curriculum of the management academy since 1898 and, with the implementation of the Bologna reform in mind, it was entrusted to the School of Humanities and Social Sciences. What at Koç is called the "core program" here is called contextual studies, on the premise that their content complements the education in the core subjects by offering knowledge about historical, cultural and societal contexts. As at Koç, the linking of the core subjects and contextual studies towards an integrated body of knowledge(s) is not subject to regulation. Professor Martin Eppler, from the School of Management, stated that he saw two different approaches being practised:

One: let's keep the humanities pure, do not marry it with management topics, just make it special, unique. To open the horizon of students into new fields; not to make it pre-packaged, but students have to work in a different manner. Two: the other part believes that we need to make sure it is relevant for students in the diverse programmes.

(interview, 2015)

Here too it is mostly left to teachers to decide in favour of either of the two approaches—or to opt for a self-made mixture of the two. Student satisfaction is gauged by regular evaluations, and in these, satisfaction with the courses as such is usually recorded as quite high, though students have difficulties in perceiving the added value of contextual studies for their core subjects. Generally, this is judged to be the systemic effect of disciplinarity on both students and teachers, as the former expect to receive knowledge the practical value of which is immediately apparent and testable, while the latter have to put a lot more effort into their teaching than at a university where they teach students of their own disciplines. Vito Roberto, professor of law and vice-president for teaching at HSG, commented that "the system rewards experts, no time to lose on integration and interdisciplinarity, if you are not specialised, expert, you stay where you are on the career ladder" (interview, 2015). Dieter Euler, professor of educational management at the School of Management, further pointed out that this put the burden of integrating different types of knowledge mainly on the students:

> We expect from students having an integrated multidisciplinary view, being problem-oriented, and all the professors are uniquely disciplinary-oriented. In general, professors are reticent engaging with issues beyond their disciplinary borders. We have a type of cafeteria system with our courses in contextual studies, where students can choose among many options, that is not integration.
>
> *(interview, 2015)*

"So it is left to the students", as Kuno Schedler, professor of public management, said, thus agreeing with several other interviewees at HSG: "They complain. 'How do you expect us to integrate and be interdisciplinary if you are not?' We are not interdisciplinary, because our publishing is in the disciplines". For him, it should clearly be the teachers' job to align their humanities content with the needs of the students:

> The challenge is to see how far-away disciplines like literature, philosophy or history can be meaningful for management. How is Chinese culture related to management? If they do not succeed in doing that, then they make themselves boring. It is a challenge for the colleagues in the School [of] Humanities and Social Sciences to try to understand how our students think and what they need for their education. How can we add to education and management, rather than being a specialist in something? Rather, what should they know, for example, of Russian culture to be successful in international business? [...] You have to get to the customer with your message. We all have to make ourselves relevant to the students.
>
> *(interview, 2015)*

Like others at HSG, Schedler is of the opinion that the St. Gallen management model developed by Hans Ulrich (Ulrich & Krieg, 1972) should provide the common body of knowledge integrating humanities and management:

> The St. Gallen management model was designed in the '60s, very inter-disciplinary. At that time, management was very functionalist, very detail-oriented and there was a lack of an overall understanding of management, a systemic perspective, and Hans Ulrich was a pioneer and a little bit revolutionary when he started talking about integrative management. We need to understand the whole of the organisation rather than just parts of it. We seem to have lost it, because international research is going deep instead of understanding the context, new methods and new technologies. It seems to me that young researchers have lost the purpose to understand organisations, to help managers to do a better job.
>
> *(interview, 2015)*

From the point of view of the humanities, this was strongly supported by Caspar Hirschi, professor of history at the HSG School of Humanities and Social Sciences (SHSS), who described the St. Gallen management model as being "packed with humanities and social sciences material", but he also is not quite sure that "what we teach here—at SHSS—gives a clear advantage in terms of management competence" (interview, 2015). Both he and Ulrich Schmid, professor of Russian at the same school and a philologist by provenance, teach with a view to relate their domains of knowledge to the needs and interests of management students. Schmid pointed out that, for humanities scholars, this required some considerable effort in reinventing at least in part the discipline in which they were trained: "All of us experience this transformation from previous positions to the life at HSG. If you're not willing to transform yourself, it makes little sense to teach at this university" (interview, 2015).

In the same vein, Vincent Kaufmann, who like Schmid is a trained philologist but who switched to teaching media studies during his years at HSG, elaborated:

> I have gone out of my discipline, I [no] longer teach French literature. [. . .] This is why [it] is so important to teach humanities here, not just because of the competences, but it is a laboratory of the humanities. How the humanities can reinvent themselves by addressing an audience. If you are in a university with humanities, you do not really have an audience, because students have to listen to what you do, because they want the degree and the job. The kind of questions we have to ask ourselves here are obviously not the same questions that our colleagues in the management and law school[s] have to ask themselves. In most of the cases, humanities are extremely conservative, past-oriented and defend themselves as

representing the past, which is kind of suicidal. [. . .] One of the issues is: what type of people do we hire? Do we hire colleagues who would prefer to be elsewhere, because they feel they do not have their own students and then they feel second-class professors? We need people who are willing to give up their disciplines.

(interview, 2015)

Quite a number of the concerns and ideas voiced about the practical side of integrated management education at HSG also resonated through our interviews at SMU. At their School of Social Sciences, SMU already has philosophy, English literature, Asian studies and theatre studies in the faculty mix. They offer elective courses in what, similar to Koç, is called the 'university core' section of the curricula, where the humanities are currently represented with one mandatory course in business ethics. In 2014, SMU established the task force "humanities@ smu", charged with developing recommendations about how to strengthen the humanities in the overall SMU model of research and education.

Professor James Tang, dean of the School of Social Sciences and chair of the task force, told us that they were currently working "with a notion of a twenty-first-century version of humanities, which is still only an idea in the making" (interview, 2014). However, there were already some outlines as to where this notion was heading: "Humanities should not be divided in disciplinary departments, but engage with problems in co-operation with other fields", Tang stated, explaining that this was why the task force was programmatically opposed to creating a new School of Humanities at SMU: "We want to avoid building a silo" (interview, 2014). Instead, it was planned to recruit teachers of humanities content with a view to integrating them into existing schools:

We want to make more choices available for the students. And we want to introduce 'joint appointments' between core degree departments and social science and humanities appointments. And perhaps we will add a new specialised programme integrating humanities, but this is not a main priority now. The 'joint appointment' approach might cut through the silo problem. We still have a problem of how to locate humanities scholars in our system. This is a university governance issue. What we hope to achieve is to be able to recruit like-minded professors [. . .] and through that have other schools enter the space of humanities.

(interview, 2014)

Asked about a metaphor that he used repeatedly in our interview—the metaphor of the humanities as a "connective tissue"—Tang explained,

The idea of humanities as 'a connective tissue' relates both to structural and learning-related aspects of integrating humanities. This metaphor was the one that found resonance in our international academic review board. This is the way we capture our approach: avoiding silos, an integrated, inter-connective sort of learning. We want to be organic in how we grow. We will also use this as a way of communicating to future faculty members what we work towards, that they are not entering a specialised department, but become part of a 'body' playing a connective role.

(interview, 2014)

As in other schools, discussion about how to implement this idea raised concerns about interdisciplinary co-operations, as Sriven Naidu elaborated,

Our faculty is still relatively young, which means that disciplinary creden-tials are important. It's a life-cycle thing for the university to grow more interdisciplinary departments. One tool is 'themes' of research that cut across disciplines (innovation, urban sustainability, data analytics, social ana-lytics). In the first round of funding, the cross-disciplinary co-operation was limited, but now with the second round more collaboration is emerging. We focus on incentivising senior faculty who are not forced to focus on disciplinarity. [. . .] The integration of humanities should help speed up processes of cross-over collaboration. Humanities could be a seed for open-ing departments more to new ideas and perspectives which can help grow cross-disciplinary co-operation.

(interview, 2014)

Professor Yang Hoong Pang, then-dean of the School of Accountancy, vice-provost of undergraduate education and chair of the University Curriculum Committee, had been part of the group which, after extensive inquiries into the needs and wishes of the stakeholders of management education in Singapore, designed the foundational curricula of SMU with their 'university core'. Being closely involved with the reform of that core according to the findings and deliberations of the task force, she said,

The common goal is to provide a holistic education for our students. [. . .] We don't want discipline-based education only. The colonial heritage of [the] British university system, with a strong focus on disciplines, is some-thing we needed to overcome.

(interview, 2014)

Instead, SMU turned towards the North American model of including the liberal arts in the sense of a general education which adds humanities content, like the history and culture of Asia, to management skills in order to improve on both personality-building and the cultural literacy of their students.

All in all, our findings suggest that there are basically four different concepts of integrating the humanities and social sciences into transformative management education: the 'general education' approach taken by Koç, ESADE and HSG; the 'differentiated market' approach taken by CBS and LUMS, offering their students the choice between integrated and specialised programmes; the 'problem-oriented' approach taken by SMU to foster cross-disciplinary collaboration in teaching and research; and, finally, the 'implicit encouragement' of emerging integrational efforts at SSE. The reasons for choosing these respective approaches vary between the schools, of course, due to their political and cultural frameworks and histories, but they have one significant aspect in common: all of them seem to be moving away from a system that they perceive as outdated rather than moving towards a clearly defined new system, which suggests that the conceptualisation of interdisciplinary knowledge transfer is mainly still at an exploratory stage of development even at schools which, like HSG and CBS, can already look back on a long tradition of practising it.

The Skills of Integration: Conclusions and Suggestions

It will have been noted by our readers that the term we have consistently used for describing the endeavour to include the humanities and social sciences in transformative management education is 'integration'. Used equally consistently by our interviewees (which is the reason we adopted it), this term carries an in-built normative presupposition: integrating something into something else means that the entity integrated into something and the entity into which it is being integrated are categorically different, separated by a chasm that must be bridged. In other words, describing the relationship between management education on the one hand and the humanities and social sciences on the other by this term means that the knowledge the latter bring is perceived as categorically different from the disciplinary domain of the former.

This chasm probably has less to do with the incompatibility of contents and more with the difference between the instrumental and the transformative approach to knowledge as such. Looking back at our second chapter, the type of knowledge associated with the latter could be termed wisdom, as opposed to the former's predilection for applicable skills, encompassing an epistemological and therefore more relational understanding of content. To link these types of knowledge and ideally to bridge a gap which in our eyes is a result of the artificial segregation of disciplines would therefore seem to require a way of accessing the wisdom offered by the transformative potential of the humanities and social sciences without losing sight of the skills necessary for the profession.

To find such a way, it would first be necessary to define the value propositions that the respective partners bring to the table—which, judging from our material, is not something which comes easily to them. In fact, it did rather astonish us to find that even those of our interviewees who are most convinced of the merits of integrated management education have little knowledge about the other disciplines involved at their disposal and at the same time are mostly not readily able

to describe what exactly their own discipline is about. In the light of these observations, we will present our conclusions and suggestions again in three steps, first
appealing to management studies, second to the humanities and social sciences
to remedy this lack of communication and, thirdly, arguing for the application of
Mezirow's ideas on reframing preconceived notions (Mezirow et al., 1990) to the
system of disciplinary knowledge segregation.

Looking for Management: An Appeal to Business Schools

It is not our place, nor within our remit of competences, to pronounce on a
set of contents and skills which could or should make-up management education's value proposition in general, and accordingly, we will not even try to do so.
Equally, since we know well that it is virtually impossible for any academic institution to establish a broad consensus about such a matter, and since this would not
be compatible with the academic freedom of research and teaching, we abstain
from even suggesting such a consensus, mindful of the fact that the constant emergence of new facets to the knowledge produced at any such institution is already a
value proposition in its own right. For implementing interdisciplinary knowledge
transfer between management studies and the humanities and social sciences for
the sake of enhancing management education, however, we are convinced that it
is crucial that faculty and programme managers engaging in such transfer on the
part of management studies should take the trouble to develop what we would
like to dub 'narratives of provenance': that is, narratives explaining what the disciplinary background is to which they expect the humanities and social sciences
to relate.

Our basic assumption here is that building interdisciplinary knowledge transfer
works very much like building up any personal relationship. To create the trust
that is necessary for a mutually beneficent co-operation, there must be some input
from all sides first to establish the positions from which the parties concerned
are acting and to find a common language in which to interact. In the context
in which our interviews were conducted, that is, at business schools, it was of
course thoroughly reasonable of our interviewees from management studies to
assume that we knew exactly what their domain of knowledge was about. Still,
the vagueness of the answers we received when we did ask about it, as mentioned
earlier, hints at a general communication problem, most notably visible at Koç
and at HSG where all students are exposed to the humanities and social sciences.
When management educators cannot or do not explain what their role in management education is, what kind of knowledge they produce and transmit, then
colleagues from the humanities and social sciences, let alone students who, it must
be remembered here, usually only have a faint idea about the big picture to which
their studies are supposed to lead, will find it very hard to connect with them.

This problem could be solved in several ways. One of them would be for the
school to make sure that new colleagues from the humanities and social sciences

are trained in understanding the basics of management education, as practised by the respective institution, in a workshop or series of workshops expressly designed to this end. Experience shows that it does not take much in the way of concrete knowledge about management studies for scholars of the humanities and social sciences to become aware of what the programmes to which they are expected to contribute actually require of them. That they would be expected and perhaps even constrained actively to learn about this requirement, thereby being given information that in the end will be vital to the quality of their contributions, would quite possibly make all the difference to their general attitude, since it would not only show them the proverbial ropes but would also act as a symbolic gesture introducing them to the necessity of interdisciplinary transfer. Another possibility would be a one-on-one coaching programme, matching a new colleague with an experienced member of the faculty teaching management studies. However, the schools go about this, the most important thing is systematically to foster both the ability and the will for management scholars to talk to colleagues who are not from their peer group and therefore cannot be expected to share the tacit consent on which peer groups usually rely for in-group communication.

Actively cultivating this ability, though, only solves one-half of the problem. The other half we observed to consist of management educators' difficulties in even realising, much less overcoming, how much of their attitude towards the humanities and social sciences is influenced by preconceived assumptions about them—which often have very little to do with what their colleagues from those disciplines actually do in their research and teaching. One example of this is the much-quoted assumption that the contributions of the humanities and social sciences to management education could or would strongly go towards improving students' ethics and morality. This is probably rooted in society's faint collective memory of the Enlightenment belief that rational thought is intrinsically moral. This memory, however, invests critical thought—one of the most generally recognised competences of the humanities and social sciences in management education—with a distinctly normative quality which has since been shown by the humanities and social sciences themselves to be part of the ideological agenda of an era long gone.

Assessing our findings on the way in which management educators talk about the humanities and social sciences, we often encountered a mixture of vagueness and clichéd notions about them which stood in stark contrast to the general conviction that they could and should contribute meaningfully to management education. This gap between an overall very positive view of them and a rather marked helplessness in defining what their contribution actually is needs to be addressed just as seriously as the creation of narratives of provenance for management education. The way to go about this would be to apply Mezirow's ideas about transforming perspectives (2009) recursively to business schools; that is, not only to students' attitudes towards transformative management education but also to those of management educators. Management educators should be encouraged thoroughly to examine the presuppositions about the humanities and social sciences that they bring to their partnership, to check those presuppositions against the reality of the specific competences offered by the humanities and social sciences, and, if necessary, to adjust their framework of reference accordingly, so as to provide the basis for successful interdisciplinary knowledge transfer in terms of mutual respect.

To do this, as well as devising narratives of provenance for management education, should not be hard for business schools. Due to several factors, most notably the combination of their relative youth in terms of academic history—which means that Humboldt's politics of segregating knowledge into disciplines did not affect them as lastingly as, for example, the humanities—and their constitutional closeness to the contemporary business community, management studies are to a certain extent interdisciplinary by nature. Therefore, they are ideally equipped to practise what Sverre Raffnsøe, professor of philosophy at CBS, describes as the knowledge economy of the future:

> With new post-disciplinary contexts, academic borders, including borders between the human and the non-human, become more like thresholds that dare us to overstep them, and bridges and passageways that dare us to build them, in order to establish a new independent relationship between that which previously seemed divided.
>
> *(2013, p. 99)*

The fact that management studies currently reach out to other disciplines (in our case, the humanities and social sciences), openly admitting that there might be something missing in their traditional domain of knowledge which those disciplines could supply, suggests that business schools are both conscious of the artificial nature of their disciplinary boundaries and willing to act on this consciousness. Increasing demands for specialisation, however, have taken their toll on management education as well, threatening to decentralise management studies to the point where they no longer have an easily discernible core of content holding them together. A huge opportunity to re-establish this common core precisely on the foundation of interdisciplinary knowledge transfer might be offered by making the ability to create "bridges and passageways" between disciplines (Raffnsøe, 2013, p. 99) into an integral part of what management studies are about.

Leaving the Ivory Tower: An Appeal to the Humanities and Social Sciences

For the humanities and social sciences in management education, the need to develop narratives of provenance to facilitate interdisciplinary knowledge transfer is even greater. On the one hand, the humanities and social sciences are in the position of the entity being integrated into an already existing one, newcomers in a field whose rules and traditions have been long since established to the point that the original players often no longer are consciously aware of them. This situation makes it difficult for the newcomers to gauge what is expected of them and how to go about it, but at the same time the situation puts more responsibility on them to work towards a mutual understanding. On the other hand, many of the disciplines covered by the umbrella term 'humanities and social sciences' themselves are even less accustomed to explaining their added value to society than are management scholars.

The working environment in which the humanities and social science scholars whom we encountered at the business schools we visited find themselves is significantly different from that of their colleagues at universities which accord institutional autonomy to their disciplines. At business schools, these scholars are seldom, if ever, allowed to train students in their own disciplines, usually contributing to students' degrees without having their own disciplines recognised on graduate diplomas. This means that they are teaching students who usually have no or at least not much intrinsic interest in humanities and social science topics as such, which thus requires teachers to work out a way of arousing and holding students' interest as well as adjusting their own terminology, didactic methods and choice of content to a learning community which has no prior experience of them to build on but has a very legitimate interest in being presented with courses to which they can relate as management students. At the same time, these scholars fall out of the academic circle of reproduction by relinquishing the option of raising followers whose future professional successes would enhance their own standing by carrying on their disciplinary research and teaching. Both factors together already make for a huge step out of the proverbial ivory tower to which Humboldt's academic model had allowed and even encouraged scholars to retreat, away from everyday reality.

Often, though, these scholars remain rooted in their disciplinary peer group through their research, and this peer group still retains some of the original Humboldtian university's spirit. Having been placed at the core of the university's founding disciplines and having for a long time been recognised by the public in that role, many of the humanities scholars employed by universities today cling especially resolutely to the conviction that it is still their time-honoured right to be recognised in their full importance without having to explain themselves. As the societal importance of the humanities and social sciences has begun to be contested over the last century, this resolution has often turned into a stubbornness born both from understandable frustration engendered by mindless institutional cost-cutting and from their less understandable ignorance of the image that they have presented to society by sticking to their disciplinary guns without bothering to make their added value to society explicit. Feeling that this value should be self-evident, self-justification by humanities scholars, if offered at all, is frequently characterised by self-pity for being deeply misunderstood through no fault of their own, thus displaying in Europe the same "sorry mixture of entitlement and penury that characterizes the U.S. humanities" (Miller, 2012, p. 11). Instead of taking up the cudgel and actively marketing their products, they have chosen to take on an attitude of huffy aloofness, in consequence losing ever more ground in relation to the fast-changing knowledge economies of the present:

> By retreating to the 'essential' academic disciplines of the humanities, the human sciences further preclude themselves from participating in and contributing to collaborative efforts in those fields that currently represent in scope the vast majority of university-based activity—and which, on top of that, represent a wide and diverse landscape of scientific activity, which, in varying degrees and with varying agendas, actually recognizes the relevance and the value of the human element in scientific practice.
>
> *(Raffnsøe, 2013, p. 97)*

The attitude with which especially the humanities still today adhere to the essentialist understanding of disciplinary knowledge, though, is thoroughly at odds with the fact that the type of knowledge they produce is epistemological and thus relational by nature.

Over the last decades, this fact has been repeatedly displayed. In 2004, the European Science Foundation's Standing Committee for the Humanities (SCH), charged with creating and co-ordinating the humanities' research activities on the European level, found itself faced by the question of whether it was still needed at all or would not better be merged with the Standing Committee for the Social Sciences—meaning, of course, that both would have to lose a significant number of their members in the process. The background to the foundation's repeated discussions of this question was that funding frameworks such as the EU-run European Horizon 2020 programme were continuously narrowing the slots dedicated to the funding of both sets of disciplines until they were hardly present any more. Finally becoming frustrated with those discussions, the SCH decided that it was time to mount a counter-attack by means of a concise summing up of what exactly humanities knowledge was all about. It took the working group that was challenged to come up with such a concept nearly three years to deliver a policy briefing, in 2007, since their meetings (chaired by Ulrike Landfester, who was then representing the Swiss National Science Foundation in the SCH) showcased unexpectedly clearly the reluctance of humanities scholars to account for themselves in terms of their value proposition to society. In the end, however, those meetings produced a consensus which laid the groundwork for an understanding of the humanities, defining the type of knowledge they produce as nothing less than a set of skills structurally enabling interdisciplinary relations.

In 2013, a science policy briefing was published by the SCH (Segal et al., 2013), the title of which, *Cultural Literacy in Europe Today*, refers to the phrase 'cultural literacy' that was coined by Eric D. Hirsch in 1987 (Hirsch, 1987), clearly hinting at its core argument, namely that the humanities, here encoded as literary and cultural studies, enhance the human ability to participate actively in cultural contexts by explaining how such contexts work. These skills relate to four major paradigms: textuality, rhetoricity, historicity and fictionality. The term 'skill' may be misleading at first sight, especially when used in connection with management education, since being taught about these paradigms by the humanities does not necessarily mean that students, having completed their course or courses, will in the end be able proficiently to apply all the techniques involved. What the humanities teach is analytical awareness: the awareness that any artefact, material or immaterial, is textual in nature, built along the lines of a logic which may have little to do with the subject it deals with but everything to do with the context in which it is used; the awareness that any artefact uses rhetorical devices to manipulate its recipient towards accepting its underlying norms and frameworks of value; the awareness that any artefact has a historical dimension impacting on the meaning it transports; and, finally, the awareness that any such meaning has fictional components, as each communication through artefacts is as such intrinsically fictional in structure but of course can be fraught with any number of additional fictional elements which are not necessarily easily distinguishable from the others.

The skills imparted by the humanities, therefore, are meta-skills: to recognise textuality and perceive its architecture, to realise rhetorical means of manipulating readers' reactions and, critically, to evaluate their underlying norms and values, to relate to historicity and to weigh fictionality and distinguish between its structurally necessary and its gratuitous components. The type of knowledge that the humanities and social sciences produce is thus a meta-knowledge, that is, knowledge about the ways and means in which human society creates, encodes and distributes knowledge. This means that the subject matter researched by humanities and social science scholars is located on a level once removed from material reality, focusing on the mechanisms that society uses to deal with it. In this, the humanities and social sciences complement each other, with the social sciences investigating cultural artefacts to determine societal developments, and the humanities researching the logics and agenda of cultural artificiality as such in any given context. Taken together, the humanities and social sciences thus enable students to understand the skills they are acquiring towards practising their profession as a device for dealing with a reality which is constantly changing in its logic and agenda and which, accordingly, also constantly changes both the core and the context of management.

Since Humboldt installed the humanities as *Geisteswissenschaften*, the concept of humanity, let alone that of *Geist*, has undergone more than a few changes and is currently going through what Sverre Raffnsøe calls the "human turn": "[H] umankind's surroundings appear to have been decisively impacted by, and therefore turned towards and intently focused upon, the human element" (2013, p. 15). The 'human element' of which Raffnsøe speaks is no longer the intellectually and morally autonomous human being celebrated by the Enlightenment movement, since the boundaries between nature and culture, man and animal, body and machine, virtuality and reality—which had stabilised the mind-set of the early nineteenth century—have become fluid and permeable, and the Enlightenment's rampant anthropocentrism has become a little-mourned thing of the past. Faced with this development, Raffnsøe suggests, the humanities should reinvent themselves as 'posthuman' humanities, engaging in the making of a "contemporary relational topography" (Raffnsøe, 2013; Braidotti, 2013).

The French philosopher Catherine Malabou offers an interesting framework in which to develop this thought further. Her essay "The Future of Humanities" states that "science" (encompassing mathematics, physics, medical science and, most importantly for Malabou, biology, with a focus on neurobiology) is "gradually becoming a discourse on frontiers, on limits, and has thus begun to deprive the Humanities of their proper content or task: the reflexion upon frontiers and limits" (Malabou, 2011, p. 1). Based on the famous essays by Michel Foucault, "What Is Enlightenment?" (Foucault, 1984), and by Jacques Derrida, "The University Without Condition" (Derrida, 2002), she argues that the humanities should repossess this "proper content", taking a leading role in boundary work, as "[t]he future of any kind of discourse [. . .], be it philosophical, literary or scientific, is linked with the plasticity of its limits and frontiers" (Malabou, 2011, p. 1). This notion of 'plasticity' is derived from a discovery presented by Norman Doidge in *The Brain That Changes Itself* (Doidge, 2007), which comprehensively undid the humanities' former claim to be the sole proprietors of knowledge about a humanity defined by *Geist*:

> I think that the event that made the plastic change of plasticity possible was for a major part the discovery of a still unheard of plasticity in the middle of the XXth century, and that has become visible and obvious only recently, i.e. the plasticity of the brain that worked in a way behind continental philosophy's back. The transformation of the transcendental into a plastic material did not come from within the Humanities. It came precisely from the outside of the Humanities, with, again, the notion of neural plasticity.
>
> *(Malabou, 2011, p. 5)*

Malabou's metaphor of 'plasticity' is perhaps an even more suitable and certainly a more consensual one than that of "sexing the cherry" with which we start the next sub-chapter. Whichever metaphor we choose, though, it has become obvious to us that, in order to develop something like Raffnsøe's "contemporary relational topography" (Raffnsøe, 2013) whereby management studies, the humanities and the social sciences can grow to trust in and even rely on each other to educate future managers together, there remains a lot of work to be done in the field of conceptualising knowledge. Much of this work, this much is clear, falls to the humanities, whose representatives we met at the schools that we visited we found to be both conscious of the challenge and more than willing to engage with it. To establish a relational concept of knowledge in place of the outworn essentialism of the Humboldtian university, however, cannot rest on the shoulders of one group of disciplines alone, and especially not when those disciplines, at many universities, are increasingly marginalised. It is true that the humanities have not taken enough responsibility for themselves and their image during the last century, but it is equally true that the need for a relational concept of knowledge must be recognised and acted upon by all disciplines concerned if such a concept is to be sustainable.

De-sexing the Cherry: The Knowledge of Concepts

Sexing the Cherry is the title of a famous novel published by Jeanette Winterson in 1989 (Winterson, 1989), in which the main character, Dog Woman, is painted in terms which subvert traditional gender dichotomies so consistently that, even though this character is denominated a woman, the reader perceives her as very much male in demeanour and interests. The novel's title holds the key to this narrative technique: colloquially, the term "cherry" is used to describe the female hymen, though the cherry as a fruit has neither sex nor gender. The author's point is that even, and perhaps especially, phenomena like a person's biological sex are not as such carriers of social meaning like, for instance, recognisably gendered role models; instead, those meanings are ascribed to them by society, turning an originally non-gendered product of nature—in this case, the cherry—into a product of culture, a construct regulated by normative concepts which are in no way derived from or even related to its carrier substance.

The point we are making here is that the knowledge or knowledges still claimed today by academic disciplines as their own are, like Winterson's cherry, not at all naturally preordained to belong to either management education or the disciplines grouped under the heading of the humanities and social sciences. To stick to Winterson's metaphor, in the shape that disciplinary segregation has given them, these types of knowledge are all sexed cherries. As with the essentialism underlying the assumption that their biological sex automatically binds women—and, of course, men—to compliance with socially prescribed role models, the conceptual essentialism underlying such claims is just as much a product of culture and thus an artefact as the role models themselves or, in our case, the traditional academic disciplines.

Judging from the material we presented in this chapter, universities are still trying to hold out "the promise of an institution that can codify and disseminate knowledge on a large scale and over a long time" (O'Connor, 2016, p. 46), jealously guarding their traditional position and thus remaining what Martin Parker has recently described as "classification machines, institutions designed to keep things separated" (Parker, 2016, p. 498). Consequently, while there is a certain uncomfortable awareness developing that disciplinary knowledge might quite possibly not be the stable, if growing, corpus of skills and techniques to be taught that it was believed to be, the habit of understanding knowledge ontologically is still going strong. This habit impacts heavily on the efforts made to find a way towards integrating the humanities and social sciences, since it obstructs interdisciplinary knowledge transfer not only on the practical but also on the theoretical level of both education and research. Thus, the main problem with interdisciplinary knowledge transfer is not the fault of individuals but a systemic effect of disciplinary segregation, up to and including the use of language itself. The more specialised the disciplines become, the more opaque their terminologies tend to be, to the point at which some disciplines' intra-language is virtually inaccessible for outsiders. While serving the unquestionable need for describing complex phenomena, this opacity raises the cost of opportunity for interdisciplinary discourse significantly, even between management studies, the humanities and the social sciences, which are still comparatively closer to each other terminologically than, for example, management studies and quantum physics.

Learning to understand and perhaps even speak the language of other disciplines, though certainly necessary in practical terms, will not in and of itself solve the underlying problem. To reach a sustainable level of quality for knowledge transfer between management studies and the humanities and social sciences, the respective partners will first have to examine critically the concept of knowledge with which they operate in their respective areas of expertise, rather in the manner which we expect of students when teaching them about transforming their perspectives. Ultimately, this could lead to a mutual understanding that the different frameworks have one factor in common, namely their cultural and social artificiality, which in turn could lead to a more relational understanding of knowledge. This understanding could create a knowledge of concepts that enables us to link the latter by creating equally artificial gateways which then would be perceived not as an imposition on disciplinary domains but rather as an extension of their outreach towards a common purpose.

Thinking of knowledge as created through conceptual construction, rather than through the retrieval of given facts, means redefining the boundaries currently organising academia as a whole (see Bardecki, 2015, passim). This applies both to the boundaries crossed by interdisciplinary teaching and research and the boundary implicit in the relationship between academic and non-academic knowledge. The concept of academic knowledge in itself is just as much a construction as its disciplinary sub-sections, separating the two sides by what is usually called academic rigour on the side of university scholars, since they are expected to base their teaching on methodologically sound and politically unbiased research. As much rigorous research these days is done outside universities, and often under financial conditions which are more attractive to excellent scholars than is the case in academia, this particular boundary has been eroded for some time now, while management studies have pushed those boundaries from inside academia from the start by their close ties with their non-academic stakeholders.

Academic knowledge, then, seems to be not only a distinctly hegemonic concept but also a rather outdated one which, additionally, is in the process of being further diluted by transformative education turning away from the object and towards students' human growth, expecting them to draw on personal experience, including emotional responses outside the classroom as much as on work inside it. Taken together with the observation that interdisciplinarity has for a long time at least in name become established as the way to improve on cutting-edge research, and in the realm of several academic fields, especially sustainability studies, "is almost mainstream nowadays" (Merck & Beermann, 2015, p. 19), this raises the question of what, if any, role such boundaries could or should play today. Bearing in mind that disciplinary segregation was institutionalised by Humboldt to keep the portfolio of specialisations combined under the roof of the university manageable (Östling, 2018), there is certainly a structural need to retain mechanisms for differentiating between such specialisations. To abolish disciplinary boundaries altogether—if it were at all possible to enforce this, which quite patently it is not—would create chaos. What could be done, however, is to work towards generally understanding such boundaries as interfaces enabling scholars to connect instead of as demarcation lines dividing them.

A strong argument for changing the current tangled web of permeable, half-permeable and impermeable disciplinary boundaries into a relational web of such interfaces is to be found in the dynamics of research technology that has been growing along with digitalisation. In a certain way, digitalisation has an effect on today's economies of knowledge similar to that which the Enlightenment movement's freeing of the human being for autonomous research had two centuries ago. Even more today than was the case then, it is impossible for any human beings and even for disciplinary communities to have all the knowledge that they might need or wish for at their fingertips, making it even more essential to reframe the concept of academic knowledge as a concept of cooperative interdisciplinary relatedness.

To sum up, both management scholars and the humanities and social science scholars engaged in transformative management education often seem to find their efforts in this area hampered by their difficulties with interdisciplinary knowledge transfer. The reasons for this lie partly in their not being used to making their disciplinary background and its added value to society explicit in a manner which can be understood by colleagues from other disciplines, which led us to suggest that all parties should work on concise narratives of provenance to make their position in the common educational endeavour transparent enough for meaningful communication. Partly, however, these scholars are also impeded by their own assumptions and presuppositions about the other disciplines involved, which is why we suggested that they should apply Mezirow's theory of perspective transformation (Mezirow, 2009) to those assumptions and check them against the other disciplines' perceptions of themselves.

That interdisciplinary knowledge transfer has proved to be the most problematic part of integrated education, even when all parties are basically in consent about going for transformative education as such, stems from the disciplinary segregation of knowledge inherent to the model of the Humboldtian university, which has proved remarkably resilient in academia on the surface but, as shown by the last part of this sub-chapter, is in fact now eroding fast. Having sketched out some ideas as to how to reframe it, we remain convinced that, however much the shift to transformative education by means of interdisciplinary knowledge transfer has to come from teachers themselves, thus placing much responsibility for its success on them, it is still, as we will try to show in our next chapter, business schools as institutions which have to stabilise this change by means of organisational and governance measures.

4

TRANSFORMING BUSINESS SCHOOLS

Strategic Challenges

From the first, in selecting the business schools that we later visited, we put a strong emphasis on questions pertaining to whether the integration of the humanities and social sciences into management education was part of the school's strategy and, if so, on what level, by whom and in what manner strategic discussions about it were conducted, who was responsible for strategic decisions and how such decisions, if taken, were being implemented. There were especially two issues which were diagnosed as seriously difficult by our interviewees across all the schools in terms of organisation and governance: first, the management of reform processes under the conditions imposed by the academic privilege of freedom of teaching and research, and second, the influence of external contextual factors, including political regulations and expectations, financial limitations not under the control of the university itself and, not least, the pressures exerted by international standardisation through rankings and accreditations.

"The Behavioural Complexity of Professors" and Other Internal Challenges

Joan Rodón Mòdol at ESADE, director of its flagship BBA programme, made it clear that he was not completely serious when he announced with a grin that, when the planned reform of the BBA strengthening the humanities and social sciences went through, one of the goals linked to the reform would be to "control a little bit better the behavioural complexity of professors" (interview, 2015). Seriously meant or not, with this statement, he touched upon a set of questions which partly has already emerged in the third part of the previous chapter: for, since universities are traditionally self-administered in the areas of teaching and research, faculty are more or less free to define what their students are supposed to learn.

Of course, their freedom has some boundaries set by rankings, accreditations and other external factors (which will be treated in the second part of this chapter), but within those boundaries, for degree programmes, the schools or departments which run them decide what their students need to be taught and, for the courses themselves, the teaching faculty do so.

This means that there is a certain operational tension between the mandate of university governance to create and stabilise the corporate identity of the institution as a whole with regard to a recognisable brand, on the one hand, and the freedom of teaching and research that is accorded to academic faculty by the Humboldtian university model and, in some countries (such as Switzerland), is even granted by the country's constitution, on the other. Therefore, while a university's governing bodies can and indeed in many cases actively do promote the development of degree programmes towards what they see as beneficial goals for the institution as such, faculty play a huge part in reform endeavours, a part which is not easily controlled or even influenced in a top-down way. At the same time, any reform project which aims at sustainable changes needs to have the backing of the institution for the implementation of its organisational structures, teaching vessels and programme governance to create a lasting effect. Thus, depending on whether the integration of the humanities and social sciences into management education is implicitly or explicitly endorsed by the respective institution and/or whether reform processes are instigated top-down or bottom-up, our interviews showed a variety of strategic approaches, ranging from 'silent' reform endeavours practised by faculty without institutional backing to reforms decisively imposed by university governance.

SSE, for example, currently favours the 'silent' approach, as the integration of different types of knowledge mainly takes place within courses, even though the Department of Management and Organisation as a whole is also openly condoning and even promoting this. As Emma Stenström told us, this is due not primarily to new ideas about management education but rather to an attempt to hold on to a concept dating back to before the Bologna reform. At that time, the department ran a programme combining the humanities with management education, which, however, did not rely on the school's resources but was financed by a foundation:

> Then with Bologna, everything changed, everything went narrow and [that] is when in my opinion it continued going on in an informal way. For the future, I am working with a group of people on rethinking management, and we are working on a track that would run through the programme which would be more explicit. We would continue to have the informal going on.
>
> *(interview, 2015)*

The Bologna reform, it seems, due to the rigorous standardising of curricula with regard to the translatable value of credit points, drove the endeavours of the department to keep to a broader view of management more or less underground and was perceived by Stenström as well as by Jesper Blomberg, associate professor of management at SSE, to be likely to remain there for the time being. It seems, however, that it was not the Bologna reform as such which restricted the development of integrated management education at SSE but rather the then-president, who implemented it according to his own interpretation of both the necessities coming with the concept of standardising curricula in line with the Bologna reform and what he saw as the unique selling points of SSE. According to Blomberg, he

> wanted to convert SSE into a pure financial university. The first thing he did was to cut costs. The way finance is taught here is very technical and specialised, humanities have no place here. "Ethics does not make our students richer or more successful"
>
> *(interview, 2015)*

this last sentence being quoted by Blomberg as one of this president's key arguments for shaping SSE according to a strictly disciplinary vision of management education. In consequence, the teaching vessels that were formerly officially dedicated to integrated management were more or less abolished, leaving, however, some grey zones in which faculty were able to hold on to, if not the vessels themselves, then at least parts of their content; since, Blomberg informed us, SSE "has always been very informal, we are not bureaucratic" (interview, 2015).

Similarly, Jan Molin, the dean of education at CBS, explained that presidential decisions have had an enormous impact on the development of the school. As he told us, the particular brand of integrated management education for which CBS is widely renowned today, especially in the Department of Management and Philosophy, had been deliberately instigated by former-president Finn Junge-Jensen who held his office for 22 years and, led by the vision of a "different way of looking at business and its role in society", determinedly enabled and promoted interdisciplinary teaching (interview, 2014).

Still, Molin, like Jesper Blomberg and Emma Stenström at SSE, insisted that the process set in motion by President Junge-Jensen drew its main energy from an institutional culture which worked bottom-up rather than top-down:

> CBS is an example of emergent strategies, never top-down strategy, except the case of Finn Junge-Jensen saying that "we want an open learning university", but even if this is said the application is never top-down, but depends on people and individual departments. We are a very egalitarian and flat organisation.
>
> *(interview, 2014)*

In keeping with this, Molin emphasised, CBS assigns an important voice to the students: "Legitimacy comes when students say what would make sense, [regarding] responsible management education to be integrated. It does not come from the office but from the students" (interview, 2014). Annemette Kjærgaard, vice-dean of learning, seconded this point:

> This is a network organisation. We follow a bottom-up approach, but now we will start also to develop some templates with processes to follow, in order to get faculty involved in these changes. Push from management is not possible. It is important to understand faculty motivations to implement these changes and then the examples are used to communicate to a wider faculty audience.
>
> *(interview, 2014)*

Underlying both Molin's and Kjærgaard's statements are hints of the tension mentioned earlier. It obviously took a presidential decision to set the development towards integrated management education in motion, and most of our interviewees at CBS showed some trepidation as to how far the current president would sustain the tradition created by President Junge-Jensen, as the former was perceived to look, rather than to the humanities and social sciences, to the 'hard sciences' for interdisciplinary collaboration. At the same time, the implementation of any reforms was generally seen as the business of faculty with strong input from the students. Top-down influence on strategic decisions on that matter, equally obviously, was not appreciated by the faculty—"teachers are contrarian, it is a status thing", Molin commented (interview, 2014), but his office was in the process of introducing the 'templates' mentioned by Kjærgaard to further faculty engagement by means of clearly defined organisational structures which are expected to grant both sustainability and manageability.

At LUMS, this tension seemed rather less pronounced. As its then-dean Sue Cox explained to us, one of the main arguments in favour of such programmes is very much rooted in the tradition of the university, which can still be drawn upon for legitimising integrational endeavours:

> OK, let me first tell you a little bit about Lancaster. It's a relatively young—in UK terms—university. Its origin was in the sixties, and at that time, the government wanted to set up new universities in the UK to cater for more 18-year olds to come to university. We had not got—in terms of European benchmarks—that high a participation rate. So, Lancaster was one of the chosen sites, and from its inception, it was very much about that interdisciplinary work would be part of the Lancaster offering. And indeed, it was dominated by social science and management—all aspects of management—and it was set up very early in the 60s, quite early for management schools,

with Departments of Accounting and Economics, which was one of the founding departments of this school, and operational research, marketing, and really, it was instrumental in the development of the university. But as the university developed, it merged into a very strong research-led university, and among the 50-year-old universities, it was in the top ten in the world. Older universities tend to be dominated a lot by their cultural history, and in the '60s in the UK, there was a lot of freedom of thought, there was, I guess, an attachment to unusual fields of study and ways of studying, and Lancaster students, at that time, were very politically aware, very socially aware, and most of them had an opportunity some time during their degree to study social science even though they were science students. Because the first year of the Lancaster degree was never examined towards the final degree, but the students had a freedom to choose whatever they wished to do. So, you see, culturally there was an emergent manner of being fairly eclectic and open-minded in what you studied during the first year of your degree. So, many students chose, if they were students of humanities, to do something in management, and scientists did something in management . . . It was really very open.

(interview, 2015)

To keep up the spirit of the "attachment to unusual fields of study and ways of studying" that Lancaster University was allowed and even expected to foster at the time of its foundation, the dean has considerable freedom to develop integrational programmes. At the time we visited LUMS, we were told, the management school was running "a BBA which, although it is within the management school, still draws on the whole range of fields we have" (interview, 2015) and was in the process of developing a new BSc in management, politics and international relations to offer a vehicle for teaching interdisciplinary problem-solving expressly designed to integrate humanities and social sciences and to be run from a new centre established across school borders. To do this, however, the dean could not draw on the university's financial resources but had to find funding outside:

We did it among ourselves—we got money for our centre from corporate actors, we set it up in-house, [. . .] we will put student interns into it, and we have it set up so that all students from campus can join this and sign the Al Gore principles of sustainability.

(interview, 2015)

Cox also pointed out that, for projects like this, faculty members were needed who engaged with the underlying ideas and that this would influence further recruitments:

So, it's turning. But to do it, you need, we need staff like Bogdan [Costea], and we need collaboration between many, many levels. Bogdan is a typical member of the Department of Organisation, Work and Technology. The people we will be recruiting will be like that.

(interview, 2015)

As Bogdan Costea himself told us, the initiation of the new programme has not met with any resistance by faculty: "In fact, the faculty across disciplines were all for it" (interview, 2015). This, however, in his opinion may well have to do less with a consensus about the necessity of integrated management education among faculty as a whole and more with the fact that, instead of reforming existing programmes, the school has opted for expanding the portfolio with an additional programme, so that teachers who are not interested in interdisciplinary teaching do not feel pressured into engaging with it.

Costea also explained to us that the challenge to run this programme successfully lay mostly in getting students to join it. Precisely there, however, he sees great potential in the integration of the humanities and social sciences, as the pressure on students to increase their employability in his opinion is an opportunity whereby management studies may be opened up for critical reflections about values, about which norms and ideals characterise the contemporary world of management and how these affect work-life in general, but also specifically the orientation of the students. A survey taken among potential employers the year before we visited, Costea told us, indicated that companies, when assessing future employees, looked for competences in four areas of interest, namely understanding new models of value creation, a framework of values which was not exclusively focused on money, environmental issues and ethics. The latter was perceived by companies to be most important due to the impact of the recent financial crises, so Costea took to using this interest as a vehicle for selling integrated management education to both students and future employers:

> The strategic way to get humanities and social sciences content and approaches into management education goes not through substantial argumentation, but through circumstantial relevance and legitimisation. Ethics or sustainability work, for example: this is a way to get in. But it does not provide the substantial contribution.

(interview, 2015)

This 'substantial contribution', for him, lies more in the area of understanding models of value creation and as such constitutes the core of his drawing on humanities and social sciences expertise.

At four of the schools we visited—ESADE, Koç, SMU and HSG—integrated management education is part of the official institutional strategy and as such both explicitly endorsed and structurally enabled through dedicated teaching vessels. At ESADE, the concept of holistic learning shaping both the knowledge and the character of students is anchored firmly in the Jesuit value system and thus is to be considered as mandatory. For the reform of the BBA, a task force was set up in 2013, when it was perceived by both teaching faculty and the business school's governance that the Bologna reform, implemented in 2011–12, threatened to weaken ESADE's traditional learning culture by standardising and structurally fragmenting management education. The task force's work was co-ordinated by Eduard Bonet Guinó, emeritus professor of mathematics, who had been at ESADE since nearly the time of its inauguration. In the course of his activities on behalf of the reform, Bonet Guinó authored a working paper, entitled *Educating Managers for the Twenty-First Century* (Bonet, 2015), which he distributed among the teaching faculty with a view to frame the ongoing discussion about the BBA reform, following it up with numerous meetings with concerned stakeholders. The task force's report itself is based on or at least strongly influenced by the Carnegie report published in 2011 (Colby et al., 2011). Among the key recommendations that the ESADE report put forth was the need for the concept of integrated management education to be anchored in the school's corporate identity as a whole:

> Improvements to the BBA curriculum must be based on ESADE's mission and vision and likewise on the long-standing teaching tradition of the Jesuit Society.
>
> The faculty, students and the whole ESADE community must be aware of said mission, vision and tradition and contribute to strengthening it.
>
> Improvements to the BBA curriculum and to all ESADE's teaching activities must highlight the characteristics of what is known in other countries as 'liberal education', i.e. an education based on developing the student's personality, character, values and responsibility. Because the concept of liberal education is not very well known in ESADE's culture, and because the term itself can easily be misinterpreted, the working party insists on the need to provide educational activities on this subject.
>
> *(ESADE, 2013, pp. 1–2)*

The suggestions offered by the task force were not immediately adopted for the reform of the BBA. After the report had been submitted, Eugènia Bieto Caubet, professor in the Department for Strategy and General Management and director general of ESADE, assembled a new management team across the school, including Joan Rodón Mòdol as new BBA programme director, which deemed the suggestions of the task force still too general to inform practical changes, while at the same time fully approving its direction towards strengthening the humanities and social sciences. The report of the new task force suggests going about this change in two subsequent steps, first modifying the existing programme and then, in a second step, proceeding to a revision of the programme's overall structure:

> The proposed change is being implemented within the current framework of the BBA. However, from 2016 onwards, a [. . .] structural change will

imply a further rethinking of the BBA programme and the political negotiations about this reform will determine the extent to which the humanities and social science subjects will gain further significance in the overall BBA structure. The BBA programme director aims for a generalist 3-year BBA with a strong contribution from humanities and social sciences.

(ESADE, 2015)

As Bieto Caubet, the ESADE director general, confirmed recently in a follow-up interview, the first step has in the meantime been completed (interview, 2017).

Koç University runs what it calls the 'core program', consisting of courses which are mandatory for all students. The contribution of the humanities and social sciences, which had been already part of the original core programme, was strengthened by the programme's reform in 2010. Instead of keeping to a prescribed set of eight courses, the reform opted for offering courses in seven so-called knowledge areas, allowing students more flexibility of choice while still keeping the number of courses to be chosen fixed. The knowledge areas defined are now aesthetics and interpretive understanding, the humanities, the social sciences, economic and political analysis, ethical reasoning, empirical and quantitative reasoning and the natural sciences. As Koç is a full university, the newly established knowledge areas cater for students from a variety of disciplines, surpassing the number of those taught at the business-focused universities HSG and SMU.

The Koç core programme is modelled on the idea of a liberal arts general education, to which President Ümran İnan during our interview with him showed himself to be strongly committed. "Education is an appointment between generations—it's a dialogue. Learning objectives are ridiculous. Knowing less is a requirement for creativity", he told us (interview, 2014). To him, 'knowing less' means avoiding narrow specialisation but also refers to a dialogical pedagogy through which students and teachers engage in exploring questions for which there are no clear answers and thus where judgement, critical reasoning and a social process of learning are key elements: "The institutionalised, authoritative fixation of what needs to be learned is a failure. [. . .] The essence of liberal education is that there is no truth to be learned" (interview, 2014).

The strategy paper developed for the reform of the core programme, however, seems to indicate that, even with the president's backing, getting faculty to engage with it was anticipated as difficult. The paper addresses this problem by explaining first that

> [o]ur proposal for the core curriculum will not necessarily create a larger load of courses for colleges compared to the existing core curriculum. However, the newly established departments and colleges (e.g., Medicine), and international certification programs (e.g., ABET for engineering) may complicate the relationship between the core program and concentration courses. Currently, the general curriculum requires 40 courses for

graduation. We understand that certain programs will emphasize students' professional training to satisfy international criteria.

(Funda Yağcı Acar et al., 2011, s.p.)

The paper then states quite clearly that both students and faculty are definitely expected to commit to the reformed programme:

> However, the core curriculum is an integral part of being a Koç student and graduate. Therefore, we strongly recommend members of our university to consider core and concentration courses in collaboration rather than competition.
>
> *(Funda Yağcı Acar et al., 2011, s.p.)*

Moreover, teaching faculty are charged with taking a hand in convincing students of the added value of the core programme:

> Additional requirements are suggested to explain [to] students the education philosophy of Koç University, what liberal education means, what difference it will make, what the core program is, what it aims, and how the curriculum is planned. One of the major problems faced in core courses is the unwillingness of students to take courses out of their concentration areas. Additional requirements aim to remedy this and prepare students to their academic curriculum with an open mind and curiosity. [. . .] It is very important to reach out to students at an early stage. Students are usually unfamiliar with liberal education and the purpose of the core program.
>
> *(Funda Yağcı Acar et al., 2011, s.p.)*

Following this, the paper becomes even more explicit: "Unfortunately, some of the faculty do not have a clear idea about its purpose and benefits either. Both students and faculty need a structured orientation to the core program". Besides such orientation, the paper also suggests improving on faculty management:

> In order to facilitate the quality of teaching in general, but the quality of teaching in the core program in particular, there may need to be new approaches to the ways the university handled faculty promotions. For example, those faculty members who cannot be promoted as research faculty can be given the option to become *teaching faculty* if they have the expertise and background to teach undergraduate and common core courses effectively.
>
> *(Funda Yağcı Acar et al., 2011, s.p.)*

The task force developing the paper, it appears, was thus not only very much aware of the resistance the reform was likely to encounter from faculty used to the freedom of teaching but also counted on university governance to support the reform by structural organisational measures in addition to reforming the vessel of the core programme itself, creating incentives in the shape of faculty promotions expressly earned through complying with the spirit of the reform.

At SMU, the decision to establish the task force "humanities@smu" in 2014 was made by President Arnoud de Meyer on the grounds that, as Provost Francis Koh explained to us, the university perceived the purely disciplinary model of academic education as outdated:

> Since the 1970s the education system has changed. The idea used to be to separate school students according to their talent for arts and humanities, science and technology, and with a clear priority of science and technology. This is shifting today. We still have a strong emphasis on science and technology, but we see more broad orientation taking shape.
>
> *(interview, 2014)*

The decision to go for the integration of more humanities and social sciences was, as Sriven Naidu, head of the Office for Strategic Planning at SMU and, as such, acting as secretary to the task force, informed us, inspired by the chairman of SMU's board, who "is personally engaged in broadening the university education in Singapore, away from a technocratic orientation" (interview, 2014).

At the time we visited, SMU was in the middle of a comprehensive strategy process aiming to produce a 'Vision 2025' to guide the university's development. This strategy process sought to deal with framing the current and expected future growth of SMU, both in research and education, while sustaining and furthering the current model of flexibility and interaction-centred learning. Yang Hoong Pang, vice-provost of undergraduate education, chair of the University Curriculum Committee and dean of the School of Accountancy, had already been part of the group that designed the founding curriculum of SMU. Having asked future employers about what they saw as necessary for students' education, they found a clear consensus on the need for broader competence profiles than those brought forth by traditional disciplinary management education, the graduates of which were perceived as being strong in technical skills, but lacking in communication skills, self-confidence, contextual awareness and flexibility in problem-solving. Developed to remedy this lack, and continuously evolving further, the founding curriculum was to undergo a far-reaching reform for which the task force established in 2014 was to provide the necessary input. At the moment, Professor Pang told us, curriculum management was hard put to promote the integration of the humanities and social sciences into all the programmes run by SMU:

> Different programmes have different opportunities in this regard. In some programmes, such as accountancy, we have an integrative project. But programmes have different constraints. Accountancy must comply with

accreditation standards in the field of accountancy. This programme does therefore not have too much leeway for more integration of humanities. But our integrative project does require the students to integrate all the perspectives which are part of their education. For other programmes which don't have strong accreditation standards, there are more opportunities. The best way is to work inter-disciplinar[il]y. This is also the spirit of SMU.

(interview, 2014)

The decisions on what is taught in degree-specific courses, Pang told us, were mainly taken by the schools offering those degrees; that is, the school as a whole set up the framework, "but the faculty within the schools makes decisions about specific courses and priorities in delivering within this frame". When asked what she saw as the major challenges of managing the curricula after the ongoing reform, she answered decisively:

Faculty. We have disciplinary research. One approach is to have faculty be more practice-oriented and collaborate more with industry to be able to offer more relevant courses for students. [. . .] We have a Centre for Management Practice to support this development—e.g. offering a course on case-writing. We also support faculty spending a summer in a company. The incentive structure has however to be changed, because we cannot accomplish all our vision if the incentives do not fit. We mainly reward—as most other universities—research, and research tends to be disciplinary. This has to be changed, and we have only just started this process last year. [. . .] Getting the faculty buy-in will be the major topic now. We have the buy-in from deans but the faculty will be the hardest part.

(interview, 2014)

Some months after our visit, in a follow-up Skype interview with Sriven Naidu and Yeing Soh in May 2015, we were informed that, by this stage, several key decisions had been taken regarding the strengthening of the humanities and social sciences at SMU: all students, regardless of their core subjects, would in the future be required to complete at least one course module in the humanities; an interdisciplinary research centre would be established; and a new undergraduate degree programme, combining business studies with the humanities and social sciences, modelled on similar programmes run by CBS, would be initiated in the autumn of 2016. Currently, the task force was working on the questions of how to recruit teaching staff from the humanities and social sciences and where to place them in the organisational structure of SMU, as it had been decided early on not to establish a school of their own for them, so as to avoid the building of a disciplinary silo and instead to opt for a centre of interdisciplinary research as a common platform for the new teaching staff who would be allocated to different schools at SMU.

Possibly the clearest view of what implementing and sustaining the integration of humanities and social sciences into management education means in terms of faculty management and university governance was afforded to us by our interviews at HSG. Having practised integrated management education for a long time, the institution has gathered ample experience with it, especially since contextual studies—the vessel dedicated to teaching humanities and social sciences, rather similar to the Koç core programme—are mandatory for all students to the extent of their having to complete 25% of their course credits there, thus impacting rather markedly on curriculum management. Integrated management education had been part of the HSG brand since its foundation in 1898, when it was decided that future managers were expected to learn languages, history, geography and selected parts of the natural sciences in addition to their business studies, and integrated management education has evolved further since then, its development receiving a boost in 2001 when, with the implementation of the Bologna reform, what had basically been a mandatory minor in one of the humanities and social science disciplines on offer was replaced by today's contextual studies.

Contextual studies, like their predecessors, are run by the HSG School of Humanities and Social Sciences (SHSS), which at the time of our visit consisted of ten full professors each representing one discipline—philosophy, sociology, history, media studies and area studies in English/American, Hispanic, German, Italian, Chinese and Russian culture—as well as a number of assistant professors—in charge of offering more than 400 courses per academic year. Many of those courses were taught by teaching faculty recruited from outside HSG, vetted, coordinated and supported by a programme committee which was chaired by one of the SHSS full professors, which included representatives of all HSG schools in order to ensure the attunement of contextual studies to the needs and ideas of the university's core disciplines, and which was aided by clearly defined procedures for proposing and endorsing the courses to be reviewed by the committee. The courses were grouped into three areas or so-called pillars, namely critical thinking, cultural awareness and leadership skills—from each of which students had to choose a prescribed number of courses; apart from this requirement, students were free to follow their individual interests.

In 2012, more than a decade after the implementation of contextual studies, the new HSG president, Professor Thomas Bieger, who had taken over a year before, began to promote a comprehensive reform of HSG teaching principles, charging SHSS at the same time to initiate a reform of contextual studies so as to define clear learning goals (among other things) and ensure interdisciplinary co-operation across the schools. Once set in motion, a considerable part of the efforts made by the task force charged with the reform process, we gathered from our interviews, was dedicated to improving on internal stakeholder management, especially among students and faculty. From the side of the students, there had been some specific criticism of the current contextual studies, having them choose freely between any number of thematically and methodologically unrelated courses within the programme's three key areas; it was felt that this system was not providing enough orientation to the students to assist them in optimising their educational goals. Even more prominent, however, was the general resistance engendered by students feeling that, as compared to the core courses in management education for which they had originally enrolled, the costs of opportunity charged by contextual studies courses were too high; before taking up their studies at HSG, few of them seemed to realise the impact that the programme would have on their overall grades. Ulrich Schmid, professor of Russian culture at SHSS and its dean when the reform process was started, commented that this might be an issue of communication:

> We know that we attract the best students for the McKinsey career fair and not for the contextual studies. Perhaps students will only become aware of the value of contextual studies after they graduate. Perhaps the university could do more by laying more open that 25% of the curriculum is contextual studies [. . .], a more direct fleshing out of the comprehensive approach to business studies.
>
> *(interview, 2015)*

What Schmid hinted at in the second sentence of his statement earlier indicates that the merits of contextual studies, though they are perceived by students as insufficiently supported by orientational measures available to them while they are studying at HSG, seem to become effective—and recognisable as such—after a certain period of incubation. Indeed, a survey among HSG alumni that had been carried out a few years before our visit showed that, after graduation, contextual studies and their predecessors were in retrospect seen as a unique selling point of HSG education and were for many alumni one of the mainstays of the collective HSG alumni identity.

The attitude of faculty towards contextual studies, even though they were part of a long tradition at HSG and were fully backed by the Presidency, was also far from unanimous. The fact that new faculty usually were unfamiliar with the concept of a management education including the humanities and social sciences tended to complicate their integration into HSG. This to some extent affected faculty who were recruited to the schools in charge of running the programmes in the core subjects. Vito Roberto, professor of public law at the School of Law and vice-president for teaching, told us that faculty newly recruited to other Schools of HSG without having experienced HSG education themselves tended to be "really surprised about having the contextual studies" and, if not openly critical, usually tended (at least at first) to be not much interested in engaging with them, while faculty who had been at HSG for longer, or had at some point even taken a degree at HSG themselves, usually supported the concept as such (interview, 2015). Within SHSS, recruitment processes as well as supporting new colleagues in adapting to the teaching of students outside their own disciplines of provenance were described to us as being really challenging, since the situation in which newly recruited SHSS faculty found themselves at HSG teaching students of management was usually completely outside their realms of experience with disciplinary academic teaching. Caspar Hirschi, professor of history at SHSS, told us,

> The challenge is to find people who are interested in what we do and who are able to teach what we are interested in. In some areas in works well, in others it doesn't. Some professors really adapt, changing their research interests and teaching subjects. Others stick to their usual thing.
>
> *(interview, 2015)*

Complicating matters further was the fact that, both within and without SHSS, there were two views as to how contextual studies should position themselves in questions of methodology and content. One view was that they should offer students something completely different from their core subjects, so as to have them cross into unknown territory, thus endorsing the attitude of SHSS teaching faculty who "stick to their usual thing", as Hirschi put it, an attitude which was not restricted to members of SHSS but also found in some of the colleagues from the core schools. The other view was that, as Hirschi explained, "the humanities and social sciences should be service disciplines to the core programmes", teaching subjects which were directly and self-evidently related to management and economics, enriched but not dominated by the disciplinary expertise of the humanities and social sciences (interview, 2015). As Hirschi's phrasing hints, debate on this issue within SHSS was coloured by faculty strongly resenting to see their disciplines relegated to 'service disciplines', though there seemed to be a clear consensus about complementing rather than competing with the core disciplines; however, as the academic freedom of teaching and research effectively precluded top-down interventions into teaching methods and content, this consensus was not seen as formally binding on teaching faculty.

The reform process initiated in 2012 was commented on by many of our interviewees, highlighting that faculty were very much aware—and often critical—of the limitations imposed on the interventions of university governance in the realm of teaching. Dieter Euler, professor of educational management at the School of Management and the president's delegate for accreditations, stated that it was rather tedious to try and, with the freedom of teaching being a privilege which no faculty member would willingly give up, to work on a bottom-up consensus, which would allow for an effective change in the overall teaching culture of the university:

> For this type of changes, wider consensus is required. The idea of the president is that we have to bring forward some incentives to create the change efforts bottom-up, but in fact nothing happens. I perceive there is no real need for change, no real motivation.
>
> *(interview, 2015)*

In his view, the main problem is not only that reform endeavours in the academic system have to rely on having the faculty reach a consensus on measures which, via decisions of the Senate, the Presidency is then mandated to implement, rendering the process both time-consuming and incalculable as to its outcome, but also that this system has serious difficulties in acknowledging and putting to use the constructive potential of friction between diverging viewpoints. Instead of trying not to disturb the internal peace, Euler claimed, the university governance would be better off recognising and making sense of the diversity of its faculty's ideas:

> This problem should be transformed in a virtue. These differences are positive, not the other way around. It is an illusion to believe you can have a clear unanimous view on the vision and objectives of the university, and then you deduc[e] from this the objectives of the school, and then it goes on trickling down. The issue is that visions are not operationally effective. They do not work in the concrete day by day, because people might decide to take them into consideration or not. There are no effective organisational procedures to make visions happen. An authentic way of strategy-building would be to observe what people do and try to compile it into a vision statement, just to describe what people do. It is not innovative and maybe not attractive for the outside world, but it describes the reality of the institution. [. . .] This is not part of university organisational culture, to get into these processes of change culture, because professors devote their time [to] other issues.
>
> *(interview, 2015)*

Similarly, Vincent Kaufmann, long-term chair of the Contextual Studies programme committee, formerly professor of French culture and today professor of media studies, asserted that, in his view, the interventions of university governance were sorely needed in order to change management education sustainably by means of concepts like contextual studies:

> This issue should be taken up by the university; you can[not] put us under pressure in terms of scientific results, how many peer-reviewed articles, etc., and on the other hand ask us to reinvent ourselves here. The university should provide other incentives, of course this is very difficult because universities can't decide about the standards of science, we have to submit, globally. I do not have any solution, for me it is a matter of [the] courage of the university. I would very glad if this university would be able to stand up against a conformist culture rather than submit to it.
>
> *(interview, 2015)*

Kaufmann argued that the problem with achieving the goal set down in the university's vision, i.e. the transformational fostering of personalities, as opposed to the mere delivery of management tool-boxes, was rooted in the as yet unresolved conflict between two different learning cultures at HSG, the one (catered to by the core programmes and thus dominating the learning habits of students) adjuring the students to acquire their tool-boxes by learning prefabricated knowledge by heart, and the other, catered to by contextual studies, driving students to reflect critically on the types of knowledge that they learn in the core courses as artefacts to be questioned:

> Maybe it is about reinventing the core disciplines in pedagogical terms. [...]
> We could work more on [these] two learning cultures we have here.
>
> *(interview, 2015)*

All in all, two major points stand out concerning the internal strategic discourse on integrating the humanities and social sciences at the schools we visited. One point is that the top-down and back-up nature of any such endeavours was perceived as being essential to their achieving sustainable results by both faculty and governance functionaries. As has been shown, even at business schools which either explicitly claimed to rely mainly on bottom-up reform movements, like CBS, or which used the privilege of the freedom of academic teaching to promote integrated management education through their courses, like SSE, our interviewees' statements reflected clearly that the strategic influence of the Presidency was considered crucial to the development of management education. Closely linked to this, the second point is that the management of internal stakeholders was seen to be a major challenge due both to the institutional structure of most universities and to the academic privilege of the freedom of teaching and research.

The more closely that faculty are involved in running a university, acting as programme directors, deans, vice-presidents and presidents and constituting a Senate which takes the final decisions, the greater the need for fostering a consensus among them before such decisions are taken, and the more time-consuming and laborious the process itself, as the examples of ESADE and HSG show. At the same time, even if a reform is formally approved, this does not automatically guarantee the active participation of faculty, as the academic freedom of teaching means that management faculty cannot be forced even to understand, much less to engage with the humanities and social sciences if they are unwilling or uninterested, on the one hand, and the humanities and social sciences cannot be given orders about how to run their courses, on the other. This means that implementing, stabilising and optimising integrated management education has to work with two different types of strategic discourse, one being the question of formal endorsement and structural enabling of it on the part of university governance, the other consisting of informal or semi-formal internal communication, with the aim of both reaching a consensus leading to formal approval and wooing the practical participation of faculty.

"We Need to Be Able to Sell It": External Strategic Challenges

"There is much appreciation of this being important, that it is needed", Sue Cox, dean of LUMS, told us, with 'it' here meaning the integration of the humanities and social sciences into management education. "But we need to be able to sell it" (interview, 2015). Cox's statement resonates on three levels. The first level, i.e. the selling of integrated management education to faculty, has already been addressed in the first part of this chapter. The second level concerns selling integrated management education to students so that they enrol in the relevant programmes offered by LUMS, an issue which is of pressing importance not only to universities whose funding partly or wholly depends on tuition fees but also in terms of reputation, since no university will risk damaging its reputation with a programme which is unable to engage students' interest. The third level, finally, is the management of the respective school's societal stakeholders, which include funding agencies, ranging from private donors to the country's taxpayers, but also the political and economic framework of the country within which the school operates. Basically, the input we gathered from our interviews was centred on four key aspects, the respective relevance of which was assessed quite differently across the schools we visited, namely the financial aspect (the issue of funding either to impede or enable integrated management education); the aspect of students' employability, as perceived by future employers; the aspect of complying with—or trying to renegotiate—the terms of rankings and accreditations from the perspective of an integration of the humanities and social sciences; and the influence of the school's own cultural and political settings on policy.

The issue of funding and its impact on integrated management education was brought up most explicitly at LUMS, SSE and CBS. At LUMS, Sue Cox explained to us that Lancaster University had been founded as a public university with the unique selling point of allowing all its students to choose freely among courses from any of its schools during their first year, thus engendering a strong brand of interdisciplinary education. However, this tradition had suffered recently due to several changes, among them the introduction of tuition fees, which meant that the university's funding had become more dependent on attracting paying students. Thus, its schools found themselves under pressure to streamline programmes into products which could be sold on an international market which was becoming ever more competitive. This in turn meant that, instead of being showcases of the interdisciplinarity with which Lancaster University was making a name for itself at the time of its foundation, programmes that were operating outside the mainstream—which seemingly applied to those offering integrated management education—needed to reframe themselves, if not in terms of content, then at least in terms of communication, i.e. their sales talk needed to convince students to join them, as interdisciplinary education threatened to become a liability rather than an asset. In consequence, Lancaster University's Vision 2020, while stressing the significance of "stimulating learning" and, in further explanations, committing explicitly to "transform people's lives and society through teaching and student experience" (see www.lancaster.ac.uk/about-us/strategic-plan/), makes no mention of interdisciplinarity either in research or in teaching.

It was evident both at SSE and at CBS that universities which were under pressure to streamline their products under the conditions imposed on them by, among other factors, the Bologna reform, showed themselves reluctant to allocate financial resources to programmes offering integrated management education. At SSE, Emma Stenström told us that the School of Management had had a dedicated programme in humanities and management, financed by an external foundation, but that implementing the Bologna reform had ended the foundation's engagement due to the difficulties in aligning the programme with the Bologna European Credit Transfer System standard (interview, 2015).

At CBS, interdisciplinary management education had been strongly promoted by Finn Junge-Jensen at the Department of Organisation, who was President of CBS from 1987 to 2009. CBS had been founded in 1880 by the Association for the Education of Young Businessmen (FUHU), an association constituted by 14 active members of the Copenhagen business community who owned and managed the school until it was transferred to the state in 1965. In 1917, FUHU added a Department of Higher Management Education, which concentrated on educating its students in accountancy and languages (Lange, 2009). When Finn Junge-Jensen took over as president, he and other like-minded pioneers made the then-faculty of Modern Languages, which until then had had little contact with the CBS business and economics programmes and which, due to fading student interest and financial cutbacks, was under increasing pressure to join in the first interdisciplinary bachelor of science degree programme at CBS in business, language and culture, which is still running successfully today; this was followed by similar interdisciplinary programmes like the BSc in business administration and commercial law, that in business administration and philosophy, that in business administration and mathematics and that in business administration and IT.

Finn Junge-Jensen's policy of integrating the humanities and social sciences, rather than leaving them to fend for themselves in isolation, had also engendered structural changes. Since 2006, CBS no longer has two faculties but is organised instead as a mono-faculty business school, which, among other things, allows its interdisciplinary programmes to meet the requirements of the Bologna reform in terms of credit point distribution. It helped significantly that, as Dorte Salskov-Iversen, vice-president and head of the Department of Intercultural Communication and Management at CBS, told us, the faculty of the Business Administration and Economics department did not "police its boundaries" as much as might be the case at other business schools (interview, 2014). In addition, the Presidency launched a number of "transformational initiatives" described in a strategy paper issued by the president in 2011, including two "departmental and cross-departmental initiatives", namely the "Business and Society

(BiS)–platform" framework, dedicated to "knowledge-production that is context-driven, problem-focused and interdisciplinary research and that deals with the complex societal and business problems facing our region", and the "World Class Research Environment (WCRE)" framework, which aimed to produce internationally outstanding research, both of which were supported financially by the Presidency for five years (CBS, 2011). The "transformational potential" of these frameworks is aimed at developing a research culture which, in the case of the WCREs, is based on a concept of interdisciplinarity that is programmatically designed to affect entrepreneurship as such, as Salskov-Iversen said:

> If we wish to encourage and support entrepreneurship, we cannot simply provide a number of new courses or start a new research project (although these activities are important in themselves). Entrepreneurship has to permeate our activities. We do not promote studying or doing entrepreneurship separate from other subjects. The better innovations for growth occur when different disciplines are engaged.
>
> *(interview, 2014)*

Although two BiS platforms and six WCREs were up and running successfully at the time of our survey, both the long-term sustainability of such activities and the further development of interdisciplinary programmes seemed by no means assured, due to budgetary developments which at that time threatened severely to limit the president's scope of action in this area. Because of this, dean of education Jan Molin was sceptical about maintaining integrated management education: "Due to money pressures, the old paradigm will win. The interdisciplinary perspective will lose out" (interview, 2014). Vice-dean of education Sven Bislev explained,

> Every year our budget is being cut 2%, because this is the efficiency rate of improvement that is expected. So every year we can buy less professors' hours. This year we reached the tip[ping] point, so we are looking to [make] cutbacks.
>
> *(interview, 2014)*

One of the crucial arguments either for or against integrated management education derives, of course, from the question of whether or not students exposed to this type of education are less suited, adequately suited or even better suited to prospective jobs than students who have gone through management education without experiencing integrated humanities and social sciences. Concrete data on this issue are not easily accessible. While most universities have some type of screening system in place to keep track of their graduate job histories (graduates' entry-level salaries being an important point for rankings and accreditations), none of these systems and their questionnaires have so far included specific questions as to the relevance of integrated as opposed to traditional management education.

However, the representatives of some schools indicated clearly that talking to future employers of their graduates yielded a certain inclination on their part to favour graduates who came equipped with more than what was perceived as the usual management techniques, even though they usually seemed to see the part of the humanities and social sciences as a valued add-on to management education instead of an intrinsic part. At CBS, Jan Molin told us that such future employers were usually rather ambivalent regarding the concept of integrated management education:

> CEOs might say that "we need people with interdisciplinary competences", with [. . .] analytical and reflective competence. But also, the same people claim that students need to be strong in classical-fundamental knowledge, for example in accounting.
>
> *(interview, 2014)*

At LUMS, we were told that the question of employability was a huge issue with students, catered to with very comprehensive career services and the close monitoring of student satisfaction levels with course-work. As to whether integrated management education was valued by graduates, there were no survey data available. The way in which Bogdan Costea, however, reacted to questions about his students' employability made clear that the issue was not only very much on the agenda of the newly to-be-started integrational programme but also on that of his department as a whole, as it already offers a fourth-year mandatory course on management in the twenty-first century, which is not only well received by students but also, according to alumni entering the job market, regarded favourably by future employers (interview, 2015).

Another major issue repeatedly surfacing during our interviews was the problem of how to align programmes offering integrated management education with the cornerstone requirements defined by ranking and accreditation agencies, since the current framework of those requirements does not recognise or evaluate input by the humanities and social sciences as such. All the schools we visited showed themselves very much aware of the problems this raised with reforming management education in the direction they had decided to opt for, dealing both creatively and pragmatically with the restraints put on them by the need to comply in everyday practice but on the whole taking the situation as a challenge to improve on the system of international standardisation. LUMS dean Sue Cox, though, who was also vice-president of the European Foundation for Management Development (EFMD), one of the most influential accreditation agencies for management education, hinted that selling integrated management education to the organisation was not the easiest of tasks: "I had to stand up and represent the whole corpus in the EFMD during the financial crash", she said (interview, 2015), thus arguing for Lancaster University's inter-disciplinary approach to management education at a time when such education was being publicly blamed for not having averted and even for having contributed to the global financial crises. Consequently, Cox was asked for immediate answers. Since, however, a management education including the humanities and social sciences teaches that education is about questions rather than answers, said education finds it systemically hard to satisfy such a request.

When asked about the role of rankings in the formulation of goals for the institution to pursue, Dorte Salskov-Iversen's point of departure was the statement that "we are not going to win the salary race", referring to the dynamics of research-driven and journal-oriented business schools competing for the so-called "best professors" (interview, 2014). With reference to being embedded in a welfare-state society, Salskov-Iversen explained, there is a broad understanding at CBS that the business school cannot be—and should therefore not solely focus upon—winning the competition with business schools abroad and making it to the very top of business school rankings, as the salary levels for faculty are simply not internationally competitive at CBS. Therefore, CBS concentrates on building its brand, enhancing its attractiveness for students and their future employers, through interdisciplinary education and transformational initiatives like the ones mentioned earlier.

All the schools that we visited showed themselves to be conscious of the influence exerted on the development of their brand and, by proxy, their curricula by the cultural and political contexts in which they were embedded, though their perception as to what actually constituted those contexts in terms of regional scope and political frameworks varied. At several schools, those contexts were seen to be defined by their respective countries, including but not exclusively referring to government agenda, and what was perceived to be both the explicit content of such agenda and the implicit impact of the school's environment on its corporate identity. CBS dean of education Jan Molin, for example, pointed out that the Danish education system was highly regulated by the Ministry, the regulations to be implemented not leaving much space for integrated educational efforts. "The education system as a whole is very good at being multidisciplinary, less good at being interdisciplinary", Edward Ashbee, programme director of Sociology and Management, added (interview, 2014), explaining that in consequence students entering integrated programmes at CBS from Danish secondary schools often found it hard at first to adjust to the demand to work across disciplines.

In a way similar to CBS, SSE was established in 1909 by a foundation for the introduction of business and management studies in Sweden, but SSE is still run today as a private university and is accordingly even more closely linked to the local business community. Isak, an SSE student with a bachelor's degree in architecture and currently studying banking and finance, told us that students were well aware of how the national culture embedding SSE—and thus embedding their future employers, should they decide to remain in Sweden—was not much used to the topics taught by the humanities and social sciences:

> The Swedish business environment is quite particular about culture; when you apply for jobs, they would rather ask you in how many minutes did you run a marathon than about a book—in fact, it can be quite suspect to talk about a book. [. . .] Art is not business, philosophy is not business, golf is business. The job market wants clear profiles.
>
> *(interview, 2015)*

Jesper Blomberg, associate professor of management, stated further that he saw an ongoing development in Swedish society which was detrimental to concepts like integrated management education: "We have become more narrow about age; socio-economical status is upper-class. Self-selection and other mechanisms are in place" (interview, 2015). SSE's mission is now summed up as follows: "The objective of the Stockholm School of Economics is to, through scientific teaching and research, strengthen Sweden's competitiveness" (see www.hhs.se/en/about-us/organization/mission-and-vision/). However, even though SSE on the surface does not explicitly endorse the integration of the humanities and social sciences, the first of the core values that was presented as underlying the school's official mission in 2014 subscribed quite precisely to the types of knowledge that are perceived to lie at the heart of humanities and social science expertise:

> SSE is a place for organized skepticism, for questioning, and for critical thought. SSE will inspire individuals to challenge established conventions. Knowledge produced at SSE will be widely shared and transcend political, national and religious prejudices.
>
> *(SSE homepage, 2014)*

While SSE's mission statement itself seems to focus strongly on national interests, at first glance grounding the school's activities firmly in the embedding Swedish culture as described by Isak and Blomberg, this first core value, listed under the heading "Scientific", marked a programmatic opening for the contribution of the humanities and social sciences which may very well explain why many faculty members, especially in the School of Management, felt implicitly encouraged to explore the potential of those disciplines in their courses.

Our interviewees at ESADE, on the other hand, asserted that, on the whole, integrated education projects were firmly embedded in the school's tradition of Jesuit principles and practices, including the principle of pursuing an interdisciplinary implementation of Jesuit virtues into education. The school's learning culture, resting on this tradition, was upheld by the school's board, half of which consisted of Jesuit voters and with which the local Catalan students strongly identified. ESADE, today a part of Ramon Llull University, was established in 1958 by a coalition of Catalan entrepreneurs and the Society of Jesus. The historical context of its establishment was a deeply constrained Spanish economy and an emerging era of post-World War Two industrial growth resulting from a trade-enhancing political alliance against communist interests between the Franco dictatorship and the USA. The formation and evolution of ESADE was influenced by a Catalan political and cultural interest in preserving and shaping its own destiny independently from Franco's regime. As a Catalan institution of education, ESADE's identity is therefore rooted in local entrepreneurial and political history, and its resistance against Franco, as well as in global Jesuit ideals of education.

In more recent times, ESADE has been shaped by globalisation, both in terms of the globalised market of management education and research and the globalised job market, changing graduates and faculty career patterns as well as the interests of Catalan stakeholders which have become progressively globalised as well. Together with and partly through the increased influx of international students after Bologna and the growing pressure of rankings and accreditations, this development, as Joan Rodón Mòdol told us, threatened to weaken the school's hold on its tradition. Rather worriedly, Eduard Bonet Guinó, who organised the work of the first task force charged with reforming the BBA programme, stated that this meant "the future of business schools is not clear. In such a context, we must be clear about our values" (interview, 2015). Achieving this clarity was becoming more difficult, though, as newly incoming faculty and students had been shaped by ideas and values different from those of the traditional ESADE. Therefore, the task force charged with reforming the BBA programme in 2013 strongly recommended, in their working paper, adhering to ESADE's tradition by strengthening the part of the BBA understood as a general education to the liberal arts:

> The reasons for deciding to highlight the characteristics of a liberal education in ESADE's BBA are twofold.
>
> On the one hand, a liberal education is perfectly in keeping with the teaching tradition of the Jesuit Society, and also ESADE's tradition, mission and values, which can be described as Christian forms of liberal education. Emphasising this model is not, therefore, a radical innovation but a way of making direct contact with certain aspects of ESADE's teaching methods and aims.
>
> The second reason is that a liberal education embraces different humanistic views of teaching and many business schools are currently actively promoting it as a way to train new leaders and achieve a fairer and more humane society.
>
> *(ESADE, 2013)*

Besides the argument that the peer group of ESADE is seen to be "currently actively promoting" the integration of the humanities and social sciences, the task force offered another argument which directly pertains to the shift from instrumental to transformational teaching and thus ties in with much of the material we presented in our second chapter:

> Universities also face the challenge of educating what has become known as Generation Y: young people with good IT skills but not such good soft skills, who are highly critical of hierarchies and traditional education, and who do not seek loyalty within companies but mentors and social networks able to improve their career prospects. In this respect the BBA program aims to contribute to the integral learning and education of its participants.
>
> *(ESADE, 2013)*

A direct outcome of those recommendations was the ESADE initiative for teaching innovation called "Student First", advertised on the school's homepage, an initiative which aims to

> renew its educational methodology in order to create innovative learning ecosystems capable of enhancing the transformational power of the educational experiences that our various programmes offer to students and participants.
>
> *(see www.esade.edu/en/about-us/ESADE-method)*

A private university like ESADE, Koç University was established in 1993 by the Vehbi Koç Foundation, endowed by the late Vehbi Koç in 1969 and modelled on the US Ford Foundation. Koç was the founder of what today is the Koç Holding Group in Turkey, ranking 172nd in the *Fortune* magazine's Global 500 list. "A dedicated and active philanthropist, Mr. Koç wanted to create a university that would provide Turkish students with a world class education", the EFMD business magazine reported in 2009 in an article on Baris Tan, the dean of the College of Administrative Sciences and Economics and director of the Graduate School of Business at Koç, who is quoted in this article as believing "that going through the EQUIS accreditation has allowed us to learn more about, and from, the European experience, as well as strengthening our ties with Europe" (Bickerstaffe, 2009, p. 10). Having started out as a business school, the university has since then extended its scope to include law, medicine, information technology and engineering. The Koç family's philanthropic and cultural interests invested it from the start with a strong leaning towards interdisciplinary education, and especially the contribution of the humanities and social sciences, which significantly shaped the concept of its core programme. The strategy paper for the reform of the programme included a paragraph which, while it clearly shows the imprint of the Koç family interests, at the same time hints at a very discreetly phrased political intention which, in the light of recent developments in Turkey, invests the passage with a certain poignancy:

> The core curriculum encourages students to appreciate the artistic and cultural heritage of Turkey and the world. While democratization of culture (making great artistic and cultural products of human achievement available) is a valuable goal, the core program also pursues an agenda of cultural democratization, illustrating the value of diversity in cultural and artistic interpretations.
>
> *(Funda Yağcı Acar, 2011, s.p.)*

During our visit, the then-president of Koç University, Professor Ümran İnan, made it clear to us that he saw the pursuit of those goals as one of the key factors of Koç's brand and that, in this view, he was explicitly backed by the university's governing board, not least because it included members of the Koç family who were still actively promoting the founder's original interests.

As at Koç, interdisciplinary education has been part of the HSG brand since its foundation. Established in 1898 by the Chamber of Commerce as a commercial academy with a view to training the managers of what was then the extremely potent local textile industry at home (in 1912, lace and embroideries produced in St. Gallen were the main export factor in all of Switzerland), the university is a public university belonging to the Canton of St. Gallen. Mirroring the interests of its founders in both the technical dimension of their production and their increasingly globalised business activities, the academy's first curriculum included, among other subjects, chemistry, geography, history and several languages as mandatory parts of the students' education. When the growing academy was restructured in 1919, alongside Departments of Business Administration, Economics and Law, and Technology and Natural Sciences, Departments of Language and History and Pedagogics and Philosophy were also established. The latter were merged into a Department of Languages, History and Philosophy in 1939, which was then renamed the Department of Cultural Sciences in 1975 and is today the School of Humanities and Social Sciences (SHSS).

In 2001, the Bologna reform impacted heavily on the SHSS. Until then, HSG students had had to choose one of the disciplines represented by the school's faculty as a minor to be pursued alongside their respective majors in the university's core subjects. When the Bologna reform was implemented by the Presidency, the former structure, in which students had to invest roughly 12% of their study time in their minors, was replaced by the Contextual Studies programme, thereby giving up on the consecutive educational structure of the minor and instead offering students a free choice among a huge number of courses in leadership skills, cultural awareness and critical thinking, three clusters or 'pillars' in each of which the students had to achieve a designated number of credit points, together now making up 25% of their overall credit points (Eberle & Metelmann, 2016, pp. 400–3). Today the school, consisting of 17 disciplines (12 of which are represented by a full professor), offers approximately 400 courses per year on the bachelor and master levels.

This massive strengthening of the contribution of the humanities and social sciences was the result of a strategic decision promoted by the then-president of HSG, Peter Gomez, and taken by the university's Senate. In 2000, shortly before the implementation of the reform started, the Senate agreed on a Vision 2005 which read,

> We are acknowledged as one of the leading business universities in Europe, in science as well as in practice. We are united by an integrative perspective of economic science, law, and social sciences.
>
> *(HSG, 1999/2000)*

While underscoring the university community's commitment to an "integrative perspective" on management education, the Vision 2005 notably did not refer to the humanities. After three rounds of revising the Vision, this has still not changed in the new HSG Roadmap 2025:

> As a leading business university, we set global standards for research and teaching by promoting integrative thought, responsible action and an entrepreneurial spirit of innovation in business and society.
>
> *(see www.unisg.ch/en/universitaet/ueber-uns/vision/hsg-roadmap-2025)*

What has changed, however, is that now the vision emphasises an element which was also notably missing from the Vision 2005, namely the significance of management education for society as a whole, which, as the General Principles elaborating on the earlier Vision's background have it under the heading "Research for Society", includes both "social and cultural perspectives". Interestingly, in these General Principles, the university also explicitly refers to its own local political context, implying (if not stating openly) that such aspects might be tied in with each other by acknowledging responsibility for its embedding in society:

> We understand HSG's cultivation and reinforcement of its roots in the city and the canton to be a central feature of our university's identity. We therefore strengthen the region by increasing its international visibility and at the same time make ourselves available locally as a scientific and cultural resource.
>
> *(see www.unisg.ch/en/universitaet/ueber-uns/vision/hsg-roadmap-2025)*

This approach, we were informed, might become an indirect path to having contextual studies entered into the criteria applied by, for example, EFMD for accreditations. As Dieter Euler, professor of educational management at the School of Management and the president's delegate for accreditation, told us, while accreditation processes usually go well for HSG, this is more or less in spite of, rather than because of the Contextual Studies programme, since neither EFMD nor AACSB as yet officially recognise their relevance for management education (interview, 2015). However, in 2014, EFMD chose HSG to run a pilot Business School Impact Study (BSIS) on the regional embeddedness of HSG, in which among other things the Public Lectures programme, run by SHSS, featured prominently as an indicator of the creation of added value for the region; whether the BSIS becomes an EFMD institution and possibly enhances the reputation of management education integrating the humanities and social sciences remains to be seen.

At SMU, references to the university's political and economic context by our interviewees obviously came from a rather different background. SMU, the youngest of the universities we visited, is a public university established in 2000, which was founded as a university for management education and research, and has since then also included law and information technology. From its foundation, SMU has maintained a close link with Singaporean societal and political stakeholders, to keep in touch with and serve the needs of future employers. This link, as Sriven Naidu, head of strategic planning at SMU and as such acting as secretary to the task force "humanities@smu", explained to us, was the reason why SMU was currently "moving away from being a small business school to a more comprehensive management university" (interview, 2014). When President Arnoud de Meyer decided in 2014 systematically to strengthen the contribution of the humanities and social sciences, he was supported by the chairman of SMU's board in being "personally engaged in broadening the university education in Singapore, away from a technocratic orientation" and, as Naidu added, by similar activities at other universities: "Also NUS [the National University of Singapore] and Yale have a liberal arts college which is over-subscribed, and so we saw that there is a demand for this, so a kind of competition impulse" (interview, 2014).

Adjusting to the demands of the international market in management education as well as the international outreach of Singaporean business culture, SMU's educational policy, as Francis Koh, professor of economics and then-provost of SMU, explained, was firmly replacing the formerly "paternalistic system" by a "meritocratic system", aiming to allow graduates to take their place in the job market on the basis of their merits instead of through their relations (interview, 2014). According to Sriven Naidu, the tradition of paternalism in Singaporean educational culture and its aims was still a factor to be reckoned with, although SMU's educational policy was oriented towards a "model of planning based on foreign direct investment" currently determining the Singaporean job market and thus the job options of the graduates:

> Today our educational system has become stronger and the economy is more and more diversified, so the central planning logic of education policy is slowly changing but still strong.
>
> *(interview, 2014)*

SMU's policy, as Francis Koh's statements suggested, was to merge traditional Singaporean education policy with the demands put on management schools by globalisation. When SMU was established, the US business school Wharton was used as a model for inspiration, thus diverging from the formerly strictly disciplinary degrees modelled on those of universities in the UK. As Professor Yang Hoong Pang, dean of the School of Accountancy, vice-provost of undergraduate education and chair of the University Curriculum Committee, told us,

> We don't want only economics or finance graduates, but our students must be able to work with a broad range of problems and for this they need many input[s] including psychology, history, literature, critical thinking, communication, etc. This is the idea behind the core curriculum. [. . .] When SMU was founded, it was explicitly framed as a university that should go beyond the British model of narrow education. Instead, an American model of education was used as a framing of SMU, the liberal arts approach to undergraduate education.
>
> *(interview, 2014)*

In the course of the reform worked on by the task force, however, as its chair, Professor James Tang explained its focus had shifted:

> Business education is at the core of SMU, being the founding school of the university. At the same time, the university has grown to have several schools, with a broader conception of business as a field which is part of a broad social sciences area, not merely a specialised domain in itself. This is a more European understanding of business than what we usually find in the US and Asia.
>
> *(interview, 2014)*

In consequence, Sriven Naidu elaborated, this meant that SMU would be recruiting new humanities and social sciences faculty mainly from Europe: "We have a legacy of Anglo-American scholars, and we want to look more towards continental Europe for faculty" (interview, 2014).

On the whole, the schools we visited all faced more or less the same external strategic challenges of introducing the humanities and social sciences into management education: the lack of recognition of such programmes by ranking and accreditation bodies, and the rather mixed perception of the added value of the humanities and social sciences in the eyes of students and their future employers, including the perceptions of the societies in which the respective universities were embedded. Probably due to both these factors, the universities differ in the explicitness with which they are committing themselves to interdisciplinarily integrated management, both in their strategic documents and in their presentation of themselves to the public. While ESADE, Koç and CBS quite openly display their commitment, SSE, LUMS and even HSG seem comparatively to understate theirs, and SMU has not yet fully implemented the results of its task force "humanities@SMU".

"Politics Is Everywhere": Conclusions and Suggestions

The statement made to us by Edward Ashbee, programme director of sociology and management at CBS, that in his working context "politics is everywhere" (interview, 2014) pointedly describes one of our most prominent structural findings, namely that the whole matter of integrating the humanities and social sciences into management education, as soon as it becomes the object of strategic discussions inside and outside the respective schools, is influenced by political factors in the wider sense of the term, which are not necessarily connected to the methods and content of such endeavours themselves. To bridge the gap between the former and the latter in order to assure their respective institutions' functioning is one of the most important challenges of business school governance. This challenge is made even more complex by the academic privilege of freedom of research and teaching, which was an integral part of the framework of values informing Humboldt's founding of the modern university prototype and in some countries (such as Switzerland) is even guaranteed as a constitutional right. It is this academic privilege which enables business schools to pursue innovative endeavours like the integration of the humanities and social sciences into management education. At the same time, though, keeping this privilege intact within business schools' local as well as global political frameworks requires that business school governance explicitly connect it to the strategic discourse of the school in question.

There are three main strategic issues which stood out in our interviews. One is the problem of how faculty who were not intrinsically motivated to participate in integrative management education could be brought to embrace it, so as to create a corporate culture that would be supportive of transformative teaching. The second issue was how to measure the impact of transformative management education and the contribution of the humanities and social sciences to it in a manner which can then be recognised by ranking and accreditation agencies. Thirdly, there is the issue of explicitly connecting the shift towards transformative management education with the help of the humanities and social sciences to the corporate communications of the respective business school, in order to provide information about its educational philosophy to both internal and external stakeholders.

Academic Governance Revisited: De-managerialising Faculty

On the issue of faculty management, we found that many researchers contributing to the debate on management education—Locke (1989), Amdam et al. (2003), Mintzberg (2004), Starkey and Tiratsoo (2007), Khurana (2007), Augier and March (2011) and O'Connor (2012), to name but a few—have made significant contributions to understanding the historical evolution of the institutional frameworks of business schools. However, there are only a few researchers, among them Khurana (2007, pp. 283–84), who have taken up the issue which to our surprise—even if, on reflection and in the light of our own experiences, we should have expected it—we found to be of such huge concern for the majority of our interviewees, namely that they perceived the main difficulty with the strategic alignment of integrated management education to be getting colleagues to agree first on the integration as such and then on common best practices for implementing it.

This difficulty has recently been succinctly outlined by Mark M. Davis in his book chapter, "Challenges Facing Today's Business Schools":

> Business schools need to develop truly integrated curricula. However, integration cannot be accomplished by simply waving a wand over a set of courses and saying "integration" as is so often the case; it requires commitment on behalf of both academic institutions and professors. Recognizing that the number of courses in any given degree program is a zero-sum game, each functional area must be willing to cede some of its current "territory" of required courses to allow integration to take place in the form of standalone course(s). [. . .] In addition, a new organizational framework is necessary that permits "structure to follow strategy". As a starting point, all required business courses should have a common designator rather than those of the traditional functional departments.
>
> *(Davis, 2013, p. 34)*

For the schools we visited, this was obviously easier said than done. The "traditional functional departments" to which Davis refers are built along the lines of disciplinary segregation, usually staffed by faculty who identify strongly with what they see as 'their' discipline and consequently, more often than not, are loath to enter into negotiations which might result in their having to give up parts of what they themselves see as absolutely essential in educating their students, when, for example, integrating the humanities and social sciences means ceding course vessels and credit points which they believe should be employed in enhancing disciplinary management education instead. And as management schools—and, for that matter, universities hiring humanities and social sciences faculty—still advertise positions requiring mostly clear-cut disciplinary profiles from applicants, interdisciplinary expertise remains a commodity that may well be desirable, but is not usually part of the contract offered, which in consequence leaves successful applicants mostly to their own devices as to whether or not to engage with it—especially in the light of the academic privilege of freedom of research and teaching, which, when quoted against integrated management integration, constitutes a more or less unassailable defence.

What often makes it even harder to implement strategic decisions against the will of faculty is the tradition of academic self-administration. Many European universities, especially public ones, still adhere to the principle that universities' internal governing bodies, i.e. the president, vice-presidents and deans, are elected from and by the faculty to serve in those functions for a prescribed time-span, after which they go back to their former positions within the ranks. Strategic discussions and the resulting decision-making processes therefore take place among peers, the elected functionaries having very little legal authority to govern their colleagues in terms of telling them what to do and how to do it, which renders reform processes, having to depend on argumentative persuasion, time-consuming and uncertain in their outcome.

There is, however, another aspect to the management of faculty which, though less clearly articulated than the problem of enforcing or at least encouraging compliance, still was omnipresent in the frequent references to there being too little time, too many administrative tasks and, last but not least, to the gap between teaching and research in terms of recognition. As Rehema M. White has recently pointed out, the role or rather roles of the academic in today's universities "have changed with increasing and contradictory pressures imposed" by a notable shift in higher education: navigating the challenges of globalisation, the ever-growing audit culture, research assessments and funding cuts which make acquiring third-party funding an existential necessity for many schools, a "more corporate face of higher education has emerged such that pervasive managerialism has altered the way universities work" (White, 2015, pp. 675–76). This fact is not easily compatible with what most academics expect or believe their professional role to be, since with "the commodification of education, there is a risk that business targets supersede goals for excellent teaching" and that "[p]roductivity and the bottom line are emphasised at the expense of meaning, causing a crisis of reality for many academics" (White, 2015, pp. 676–77).

For business schools, White's diagnosis probably hits even closer to home than for most other academic institutions. Where they still adhere to the Humboldtian principle of autonomous self-administration by electing presidents, deans and other governance functionaries from the ranks of their own faculty, such functionaries then find themselves in a position where they may well feel called upon to practise what they preach and research—which is, of course, management.

This means that, however much they may be consciously aware of the differences between running an academic institution and running a business, the line dividing the two organisational formats would be much less distinguishable than, say, in the case of a medical doctor called upon to preside over a medical school, since the latter would probably find it much harder to apply his or her professional knowledge to her or his governance duties than scholars of management studies would find it to apply theirs. In consequence, the governance of business schools is likely to accept and act on the "pervasive managerialism" shaping contemporary higher education (White, 2015) more readily than would other academic institutions, which in turn feeds back into the attitude of faculty towards ventures taking them out of their disciplinary comfort zones by supposedly threatening their managerial efficiency.

Under the combined circumstances of habits of mind-set by the academic culture of disciplinary segregation, the privilege of the freedom of teaching and research and the growing pressures and complexity of the academic's role(s), it is therefore not surprising that faculty at business schools should cling to their disciplinary identity in the name of the freedom of teaching and research in order to meet the expectations heaped on them by the "increasingly neo-liberal context" that White describes (2015, p. 677). By those who are not *per se* interested in shifting management education towards a more transformative mode with the help of the humanities and social sciences, being asked to assist with this may well be seen as adding yet another weight to their already gigantic workload without any benefit that they can see. Enforcing compliance with such top-down shifts would therefore only add to the sense of grievance that academics today habitually display towards reforms, putting their backs up and, even worse, if successful, eroding the freedom for research and teaching to an extent which in the long run would put the very existence of academia into serious peril.

To work towards the genuine compliance of faculty, therefore, other measures need to be considered, starting with the processes of recruiting new faculty. One of the long-term effects of Humboldt's system of disciplinary segregation—which, it will be remembered, was incidental rather than vital to his concept of the modern university—was the emergence of organisational structures which over the years have hardened into what at the schools we visited were often described by using the metaphor of a 'silo'. Both in its architectural shape and in content, the silo is the heir of and successor to the metaphor of the 'ivory tower' which, originally taken from the Bible to evoke the unworldliness of clerics' scholarly studies, became during the second half of the nineteenth century a byword for university scholars' seclusion from non-academic reality, a byword whose connotations during the twentieth century, as the added societal value of academic scholarship found itself questioned ever more critically, ripened into the near-insult it is today (Shapin, 2012). The use of the 'silo' metaphor by our interviewees was aimed not so much at the perceived-to-be-missing connection between scholarship and reality but rather at disciplinary seclusion within academia.

The organisational structure of universities and therefore also of academic business schools still very much adheres to the principle lying at the root of what the metaphor of the silo describes; that is, scholars are sorted into disciplinarily dedicated schools and departments according to the—assumed or factual—closeness of their subject matter and methodologies, the mechanisms of such disciplinary sorting having been handed on from generation to generation for so long that by now they are more or less treated as a law of nature by university governance rather than as the organisational artefact they in fact are. In consequence, by sticking to the traditional mode of having schools and departments denominated in terms of disciplines, universities still structurally encourage the habit of intellectual intra-disciplinary incest, which renders their scholars at best ill-prepared for and at worst incapable of interdisciplinary relational education.

In the light of the material we gathered, the interviewees at each school we visited were very much aware of how much these organisational structures impact on the project of relational interdisciplinary management education. Some schools, like CBS, approach the problem by creating departments and platforms dedicated to interdisciplinary management education, indexing such departments for the disciplines they have combined and leaving students free to choose either the programmes run by those departments or others offering the more traditional type of management education; others, like HSG, opt for the mandatory participation of all students in education offered by the humanities and social sciences, with its School of Humanities and Social Sciences charged with running the Contextual Studies programme. Both these concepts have no precedent in the history of management education and indeed, as with any of the other organisational practices of interdisciplinary management education that we encountered, therefore often have to struggle with sluggish opposition from colleagues and administrators alike, which is caused much less by concrete arguments than by the ingrained persistence of institutionally endorsed conventions. To deal with this, SMU has already decided that they would not create a dedicated school for the humanities and social sciences but rather integrate the scholars they plan on hiring into the existing schools, with a view to fostering problem-oriented interdisciplinary teaching and research.

In our eyes, the key to creating institutional structures to accommodate relational management education is to create structures that are flexible enough to allow for the bottom-up development of interdisciplinary co-operation while at the same time in some measure compelling faculty to engage in it. As business schools' organisational structures differ from each other according to their individual history and other factors, it makes no sense to prescribe one organisational concept above all others. Whether an institution sticks to the segregation of schools and departments for pragmatic reasons—Humboldt did have a point there—or whether it decides to go radical, and forthwith to offer only integrated programmes and to group faculty into entities according to their participation in those programmes, must of course remain the choice of these institutions. The critical factor in any structural change, however, will be the same everywhere. Business schools' governance must stand firmly and explicitly behind the strategic decision in favour of relational management education and consequently must be prepared to implement measures which secure the compliance of all parts of the school, measures which might include, for example, prescribing member-ship in several departments for faculty instead of letting scholars remain lethargi-cally bound to only one throughout their academic lives, alternatively compelling them to join an interdisciplinary research centre or to take responsibility for part of an integrated programme.

Recruiting—and retaining—faculty for transformative management education is of course the key factor for its sustainable implementation. Since full professors, at least in Europe, are mostly employed with a view to long-term stability—though even they have become significantly more mobile globally—the target group to be concerned about here is mostly that of senior lecturers, associate professors and assistant professors with or without the option of the tenure-track, as they have to be more careful about accepting positions which add credibility to their résumés in view of future appointments. Thus, they are more prone to opportunism with regard to the effects of disciplinary segregation which are still setting the qualification standards for academic employment, while at the same time they are the most likely group to move from one university to another and are as such, in some way, the fabric which keeps the global business school com-munity interlinked. Recruiting them for—and actively socialising them into—a business school committed to transformative education therefore means devising recruitment processes which, while offering credible perspectives for enhancing their disciplinary identity, equally credibly assess their potential for interdiscipli-nary co-operation.

The squaring of this particular circle will cost business schools' recruiting com-mittees the one resource of which they are notoriously short, that is, time: time to experience candidates' teaching and to evaluate it in co-operation with students, time to discuss the principles of relational teaching and to assess candidates' will-ingness to engage with them, time to introduce them into the respective business school's corporate culture and to gauge their responses to it in a way which makes the final decision meaningful to all parties concerned—time which, if reckoned up, will probably run to at least one day for each candidate selected to be in the last round of evaluation. We are well aware that this may seem a perfectly absurd proposition, as appointment committees—especially when they have to rely on outside experts—are hard put to organise even the mandatory three or four com-mittee meetings with everyone on board, which makes organising what may well amount to a week of assessment meetings with candidates into something akin to grasping for the impossible.

There is a practical way around those impracticable impositions on appoint-ment committees' resources. Business schools being what they are, that is, schools run on business as much as on academic principles, it would be perfectly viable to out-source some of the more time-consuming parts of recruiting to profes-sional assessment centres. Seeing that much of the quality development work that academic business schools pursue regularly and usually with the help of in-house teams is performed in constructive dialogue with accreditation and ranking agen-cies which are not in and of themselves part of the university, there is no rational reason why outside agencies could not be charged with tasks supplementary to the appointment of faculty. Of course, the division of labour between such an agency and the appointment committee would have to be clearly defined, and the final decision would unquestionably rest with the committee, but at least in this way the process would cost more money (sorry, bursars) than time.

Another possible measure would involve taking the admittedly revolutionary step of advertising faculty positions non-denominationally, that is, without disci-plinary markers but instead with a clear focus on having applicants explain what exactly they think they have to offer to the recruiting institution. This measure is designed to cater to a market beginning to realise that rushing after global stand-ardisation has the unwelcome side effect of ultimately producing an equality that leaves 'excellent' business schools indistinguishable from each other, thus reducing excellence to mediocrity. Slowly becoming aware of this systemic trap, business schools all over the world are beginning to look to both the embedding culture from which they have grown and their individual corporate culture in order to provide unique selling propositions to both students and faculty and to comple-ment and enhance their global credibility. The non-denominational advertisement of positions would certainly aid in having candidates commit to their future work-ing environments explicitly and constructively. However, to make sure that such a practice would enhance rather than impair a business school's international reputa-tion, it would be necessary to work out a system for quality management which translates the consequences of such practices efficiently into terms which would be recognised officially by, for example, ranking and accreditation agencies—which in turn would in all probability make faculty as a whole much more amenable to accepting the concept of transformative management education.

Quality Management Revisited: Measuring Literacies

The tools currently used in the extraction of data for quality management in busi-ness schools are as yet not well suited to evaluating transformative management education in a standardised manner, let alone the contribution of the humanities and social sciences to it, as they usually follow the logics of instrumental teaching and learning. In consequence, business schools which engage in such education display something like a blind spot in this area, which they can ill afford at a time when students refer more and more to rankings for their choice of the business school at which they want to study. At the same time, faculty—especially those who are not actively engaging with interdisciplinary teaching but, at least at some level, must support the idea of it if a school wants to establish it sustainably—will obviously find it hard to take interdisciplinarity seriously when it is not relevant to their school's rankings and accreditations, since the latter are becoming ever more vitally important to gaining and maintaining global status as a business school (Hedmo, 2004). Therefore, it is crucial to the future of transformative management education to develop standardised procedures for measuring its learning outcomes, not only in order to put a hitherto dormant capital to use but also to convince faculty to support it, in their own concrete interests and in improving on their school's official reputation.

Instrumental teaching and learning tends to be mainly teleological, expecting students to reproduce a pre-set corpus of knowledge in their final examinations. The evaluation of transformative teaching and learning, in addition to this, also needs to gauge the process of transformation by ascertaining the mind-set with which students enter the course or programme and, in the end, by measuring their progress against their point of departure, as Jack Mezirow in the final passage of *Transformative Dimensions of Adult Learning* pointed out,

> Evaluation of gains made as a result of transformative learning should attempt to map the learner's initial meaning perspective and compare it with his or her later meaning perspective. Differences analyzed should include changes in interests, goals, awareness of problems, awareness of contexts, critical reflectivity and action, openness to alternative perspectives, ability to participate freely and fully in rational discourse, and willingness to accept consensual validation as a mode of problem solving in communicative learning.
>
> *(Mezirow, 1991, p. 226)*

In practice, such evaluations have mainly been implemented by using students' autobiographical narratives. While so far this approach has been investigated mostly with regard to the education of teachers (Cranton & King, 2003; Kligyte, 2011), Nina Namaste has recently published a paper entitled "Designing and Evaluating Students' Transformative Learning" which offers a number of helpful practical insights into how to go about using such an approach with undergraduate students (Namaste, 2017). Namaste's study is based on a course she taught accompanying 18 second- and third-year students at her Canadian home institution during a semester-long study in Costa Rica. In terms of content, she was concerned with teaching intercultural competence to her students, and her goal was not only to impart knowledge but also to support students in a transformational experiencing of a foreign culture, which in turn led her to develop a matrix for measuring their progress. The documentation she used for this were the essays with which her students applied for the course and then the essay which she tasked them to write at its end, additionally referring to a weekly blog she had set up for the students to discuss their current experiences. The rubric she came up with measures four learning goals—knowledge, skills, habits of mind and action—according to five processual steps: the initial *status quo* or baseline, the minimal understanding of the issue or benchmark, the first milestone of acceptance, the second milestone of adaptation and, finally, proficiency in working with the results of the former steps (Namaste, 2017, pp. 18–19).

Taking Namaste's evaluation rubric as a starting point, we set ourselves to developing a matrix which would allow the establishment of clear criteria for evaluating students' transformational progress. Our approach to this was informed by both strategic and practical considerations. Most business schools have their own units of quality management to keep up with the demands of rankings and accreditations, as well as with monitoring course and programme quality, using well-established evaluation procedures and formats. To change those procedures for a whole school or even just for one of the programmes that it ran would require a framework of criteria which reflects the contribution of the humanities and social sciences to management education in a way—and this was the tricky part—that would ideally be generally applicable even to courses which were not designed explicitly to be taught by or even to include the humanities and social sciences, but were taught at business schools where the integration of the humanities and social sciences was practised on the strength of their help with transformative education. At the same time, this framework would need to be easily manageable, so as to make its advantages immediately evident and to minimise faculty resistance to adopting it.

The Critical Management Literacy© (CLM) framework we came up with defines its overall learning goal as students' capability actively to relate the concepts of management with which they started to the competences taught to them during their course-work. To set up what we call the Critical Management Literacy© framework, we defined four general learning goals or types of literacy:

1. Conceptual Management Literacy: Reflecting about management as a concept;
2. Cultural Literacy: Recognising the agenda behind given cultural artefacts (for instance, textbooks on management) through identifying their historical situatedness, their rhetorical devices and their relation to their specific contexts of use;
3. Social Literacy: Recognising the way in which management is connected with and influences society as a whole and reflecting on the ethical implications of this connection;
4. Interactional Literacy: Intercultural and interdisciplinary knowledge transfer, ability in team-work and constructive contributions to the learning partnership between teacher and students.

These learning goals are to be pursued in three steps or modes which, based on the three models of curriculum evaluation outlined by John P. Miller and Wayne Seller (1985), we call the transmission mode, the transaction mode and the

	Transmission	Transaction	Transformation
Conceptual Management Literacy	\<Relevant course material\>	\<Cooperation formats\>	Content mapping and reframing
Cultural Management Literacy	\<Relevant course material\>	\<Cooperation Formats\>	Content mapping and reframing
Social Management Literacy	\<Relevant course material\>	\<Cooperation Formats\>	Content mapping and reframing
Interactional Management Literacy	\<Relevant course material\>	\<Cooperation Formats\>	Content mapping and reframing

Initial Learning Perspective
Benchmark
Final Learning Perspective

FIGURE 4.1   The Critical Management Literacy

© *framework:* The Assessment Cube.

transformation mode. The transmission mode is the part of the course where students take in the course materials relevant to the topic under discussion, the transaction mode is the part in which students co-operate on assignments and present them in the classroom and the transformation mode is the part where students interlink the topics covered in the course sessions with each other, an activity we call "content mapping", connecting the course materials by identifying similarities and differences between them and thus becoming aware of the multiplicity of perspectives with which they are confronted. Progress is monitored by having students send in a short essay on what they expect from the course, based on its description, from the point of view of their respective majors, during the week before the course starts, parts of which essay are then discussed in the first kick-off session; by having them deliver a group paper based on their group presentation, at half-term; and, finally, by setting them an exam in which they are asked to compare several of the texts they have read along the logics of the "content mapping" conducted in class during the last three weeks of the course.

All in all, the CML framework is a tool with three specific purposes: (1) it serves as a matrix for course structures which clarifies the relationship between management education and the humanities and social sciences, designed as an orientational help for both teachers and students; (2) it defines the process of evaluating students' progress in transformational learning and, as such, can also be used to develop an evaluation questionnaire for student feedback on the respective course; (3) it defines learning goals which can be fed into ranking and accreditation processes.

To gather critical feedback on this tool, we presented it at the conference *The Business of Teaching* which the Aspen Undergraduate Consortium, together with

CBS, hosted in June 2018 in Copenhagen. Twenty-five colleagues from renowned business schools world-wide joined us there for a workshop in which we introduced them first to the framework and its background in our research and then to our plan for testing it. In preparation for the conference, all of us had received two course syllabi, one of them being the syllabus of the course Why Business?, taught at Wake Forest University, the other being that of the course Business, Society and Ethics, taught at Boston University. Splitting into two break-out groups, we asked the groups each to look at one of those syllabi through the lens of our framework. Specifically, we asked them to discuss the syllabi as texts, looking for signs of historical situatedness, implied frameworks of values, the way student-teacher interaction was prescribed and especially what concept of management they found underlying the course descriptions.

The ensuing discussions were both lively and very fruitful. After a certain initial astonishment about being asked to read syllabi as texts, that is, in terms of how they were constructed and how they were supposed to act on their readers, the group came up with a number of insights which showed that, in each of the two syllabi, there were indeed distinct concepts of management to be made out and that in one case this concept was even clearly, if implicitly, connected to the financial crisis of 2008 and its aftermath. As such, these insights perhaps might not be ground-breaking news, but the result that mattered to us here was the fact that, for the whole group, working with the literacies from our framework did indeed make them perceive facets of the texts whose existence they had not realised before but which, once seen, became perfectly evident and worthy of further consideration.

This consideration led to several critical observations on the concept of management education as mirrored in the two syllabi. Discussing the material used in the courses such as case studies or textbooks as cultural artefacts provoked the thought that such material usually serves to illustrate a given theory and thus offers models of problem-solving, while transformative education is supposed to open problems up for reflective inspection, provoking questions rather than answering them und helping students to find their own answers. Expanding on this, our colleagues voiced the suspicion that the emphasis laid on extensive textbook readings as the basis for any kind of classroom work, i.e. still in the largely dominant transmission mode, misses the point of addressing students' transformative potential by failing to involve them personally. Textbook readings certainly are and probably will remain necessary for the academic claim to rigour and relevance, but classroom work on such readings should focus less on the transmission of content and more on connecting students to it through reflective questions like "What is my role in this?" or "Is the argument proposed viable in the light of my own experience?", in order to foster deeper understanding of the issues in question. Taking this thought further, our group argued for focusing even more strongly on students' experiences by engaging with the materiality of everyday communication, that is, by employing visual material but also objects such as food or clothes to show how, in the case of Boston University, business, society and ethics work together, reaching out, for example, to academic approaches, such as cultural studies, materiality studies or ethnology.

At least as interesting for us as these observations was a point which we had not expected at all. Discussing the question as to whom the syllabi were addressed, the teaching faculty present soon came to the rather surprising conclusion that, in their experience, syllabi were not written for students; the general consensus was that students do not read them anyway. Instead, it turned out that our group viewed syllabi as being written both for other faculty members, so as to show them what was being done in the course and to codify learning outcomes with a view to rankings and accreditations. Judging from this, it seems that syllabi are a medium of intra-academic communication which is far more relevant to the teachers, on the one hand, and the respective schools' quality management, on the other, than to students themselves.

Apart from all the other invaluable input we received at Copenhagen, this latter point struck us forcibly as showing a way in which to put transformative management education conducted with the help of the humanities and social sciences onto the radar of ranking and accreditation agencies: if course syllabi are already written with a view to serving the demands of such agencies for relevant data, then they are the medium through which to plead the case for recognising the contribution of the humanities and social sciences. That the long-term efficiency of creating syllabi along those lines (be it through our CML framework or any other form of providing the structured assurances of learning that are necessary for the official recognition of this contribution) heavily depends on strong top-down support goes without saying. Still, writing syllabi is essentially the teaching faculty's job and, as such, it offers a viable option for bottom-up initiatives to influence the institutional response to rankings and accreditations.

To realise this—and, of course, to act on it—is all the more important for business schools engaging with the humanities and social sciences, since the references that were made during our site visits to these disciplines being *per se* incompatible with the criteria of ranking and accreditation agencies are, plainly said, based on nothing but a myth. The one kernel of truth in this myth is that ranking and accreditation agencies cannot base any decisions on the type of nebulous assertions of self-evident importance that are usually associated with the humanities in particular. If and when the humanities and social sciences put forward their contribution to management education by defining learning goals and evaluation processes, however, there is nothing to stop them from becoming part and parcel of the portfolio of achievements that business schools present to agencies for being ranked or accredited.

Quite a number of elements of management education, though not always identified as to their provenance, already come from the humanities' and social sciences' domains of knowledge, and it would not take much to make this visible. At the same time, looking at the criteria that agencies like EFMD and AACSB define for business schools' eligibility for accreditation by them clearly shows that, in fact, there is room to spare within them to accommodate the explicit integration of the humanities and social sciences. Although neither EFMD nor AACSB mentions either transformative management education as such nor the humanities and social sciences, the frameworks in which they operate allow and, especially in the case of AACSB, could even be assumed to invite an explicit showcasing of the humanities and social sciences. For instance, the preamble of AACSB's recently updated *Eligibility Procedures and Accreditation Standards for Business Accreditation* includes the following passage:

> AACSB acknowledges and values the diversity among its membership, but it also recognizes that all of its accredited members share a common purpose—the preparation of students for meaningful professional, societal and personal lives. Effective business education and research can be achieved with different balances of academic and professional engagement. However, quality business education cannot be achieved when either academic or professional engagement is absent, or when they do not intersect in meaningful ways. Accreditation should encourage an appropriate intersection of academic and professional engagement that is consistent with quality in the context of a school's mission.
>
> *(AACSB, 2017, p. 2)*

Read in the light of the material that we presented in the previous chapters, this passage and the principles of evaluation derived from it, in our eyes, is little less than a commitment to transformative management education without using the term as such. As to the humanities' and social sciences' contribution to such education, the initiative to elaborate on it explicitly in the self-assessment reports submitted by business schools would seem to us to be covered by the strong emphasis that AACSB places on visible coherence between the respective school's mission and the educational philosophy employed to operationalise it. In other words, if and when a business school decides that the purpose of "the preparation of students for meaningful professional, societal, and personal lives" (2017, p. 2) is best served by including the humanities and social sciences in management education, the school only needs to say so—which places the proverbial ball, for all its having been conveniently passed to accreditation and ranking bodies, right back in the court of business schools' own strategic responsibility for linking transformative management education with the help of the humanities and social sciences explicitly to their brand.

Business Schools' Branding Revisited: Showcasing Transformative Management Education

While reviewing our material it was a constant source of wonder to us that even those business schools which officially endorsed relational management education shy away from linking this explicitly to their school's brand as codified in, for example, their visions and mission statements. Basically, transformative interdisciplinary teaching is treated as something in between a self-evident process of emergence and a kind of bastard child who is quietly acknowledged and even provided for financially but not yet officially accorded any hereditary rights. It is our considered opinion that this leaves a rich potential untapped, the realisation of which would help with managing both internal and external stakeholders probably at least as efficiently as do the laying down of corporate educational principles and the recalibrating of quality management, provided all three could in the end be brought together in a solid corporate communication strategy.

Standing out in our discussions with students, as well as with teachers, programme directors and deans, is the need to have convincingly explained to students exactly why they are exposed to transformative learning experiences and what they are supposed to do with them. While this might at first glance look like yet another spin-off of the habits of instrumental learning, it is nonetheless a legitimate concern, especially where, as at Koç and HSG, it is mandatory for all students to engage with the humanities and social sciences and moreover, as was the case at both schools, not only students but also teachers themselves brought up the issue. Mainly, it was felt that students were overburdened with making sense of interdisciplinary interaction by themselves without receiving conceptual information on how to deal with it. It is obviously not enough to offer such interdisciplinary education as such and neither are students satisfied with formulas like "integrated problem-solving" or "holistic education" when there is no explanation to be had of what exactly integrated problem-solving and holistic education are supposed to be.

Such conceptual information is not easy to come by at the schools we visited; we are reminded here, for instance, of what Dieter Euler at HSG said about the "cafeteria system" of contextual studies (interview, 2015), whereby students choose from a broad variety of courses without receiving orientational help with this either from the teachers of the core subjects or from those teaching context courses, let alone from programme managers or administrators. Indeed, most of the schools we visited did not display their interdisciplinary endeavours towards transformative education in their visions and principles, or if they did so, only fleetingly, so that students who enter those schools are to some extent blind-sided by the experience of other disciplines' contents—their first philosophy course hitting them "like a train", as the president of Koç University expressed it (interview, 2014)—and then understandably complain about not having known what they had let themselves in for by their choice of school.

For students, this state of affairs is not ideal. Neither, for that matter, is it ideal for teachers, since students often react to the lack of orientation by resorting to opportunistic credit-point-harvesting behaviour, choosing not from interest but according to which courses seem to cost the least work, which in turn exposes teachers to the frustrating experience of students who are not able to show even the most basic intrinsic motivation for their subject. Therefore, on all accounts it would make sense for business schools which work with the humanities and social sciences to devise and distribute systematically a set of arguments, rather in the manner of a corporate branding narrative, which spells out the idea or ideas behind interdisciplinary management education, a narrative that is not only coherent in itself but also relates directly to the school's respective visions and thus defines a framework of reference for students as well as for teachers.

At the same time, such a branding narrative would be extremely useful for dealing with external stakeholders, by displaying a purpose which goes beyond merely providing students with skills on sale to the highest bidder. As Daniel LeClair has recently pointed out in a book chapter called "Prospects for Fusing Liberal Learning and Business Education in the Changing Environment of Higher Education", there already are clear indications of a shift in this direction:

> Despite the market pressures, there are signs that universities are taking on broader social problems, putting the needs of society at the center of their mission. In the wake of the Great Recession many business schools, in particular, are rediscovering their underlying social purpose. Many of those business schools are tired of being type-cast as career factories, places where people go to maximize the chances of getting their first job or next promotion.
>
> (LeClair, 2013, p. 255)

Since the integration or, as LeClair has it, the 'fusing' of the humanities and social sciences with management education is already well under way at the schools we visited and is explicitly linked by both faculty and governance to the respective school's social purpose, showcasing this integration through a corporate branding narrative which actively advocates the way in which the school works towards this purpose would not cost much more than strategic determination. This, as LeClair states, would also help with counteracting the levelling effects that the global standardisation of management education has on business schools' individual profiles:

> The lessons for management educators, including organizations such as AACSB International, are straightforward. First and foremost, to foster deep, broad-based education in business, it is most important for business schools to articulate clear, distinctive missions defining their purpose in society. Schools should stick to their missions even in the face of market pressures to conform.
>
> (LeClair, 2013, p. 259)

One last point struck us as increasingly important in this context. Already well aware of the levelling effects mentioned earlier, many business schools are turning to the culture in which they are embedded and from which they have grown, accessing their respective historical, social and political frameworks for the development of unique selling points. All the schools we visited linked their current corporate development firmly to their school's respective individual traditions: SSE underlined the connection of their integrational endeavours to their strong roots and, indeed, to their identification with their home country, Sweden; CBS pointed to equally strong roots in the Danish community; LUMS cited its tradition of interdisciplinary teaching and research established in the 1960s; ESADE adheres to the values of its Jesuit founders; Koç similarly anchors its promotion of interdisciplinarity in the values represented by the Koç family who founded them; HSG quotes its founding curriculum of 1898 when the founders, from the local textile industry, insisted on having students educated in languages, history, geography and even chemistry and engineering; at SMU, interdisciplinarity is not only equally linked to its foundational commitments but also to its emancipation from the academic system that had been imported into Asia by British colonialism; at all these schools, those links were perceived to be at the root of their turning to the humanities and social sciences for the enhancement of transformative management education. Brand narratives using this connection could help not only with selling the respective business school's educational philosophy to ranking and accreditation agencies, as well as to potential students and faculty, but also to ensure that the school is backed up by the local, national, European and even global community in which it is embedded.

To sum up, meeting the strategic challenges posed by the integration of the humanities and social sciences into transformative management education in light of the material we collected would mean to revisit faculty, quality and brand management in a manner which ultimately would have to create a strong corporate identity which explicitly includes the contribution of the humanities and social sciences. It is, quite plainly, not enough on the part of governing bodies to allow this contribution to happen, turning a blind eye to the structural and orientational needs following in the wake of its bottom-up emergence. Neither is it enough to decide on the integration of the humanities and social sciences top-down, without providing for the structural and orientational needs of both students and faculty. The shift of paradigm signalled by business schools turning to the humanities and social sciences which we have tried to map out in our report affects the very institutional fabric of contemporary academic management education. The type of knowledge offered by the humanities and social sciences, when introduced into management education, cannot, as soon as it has begun to touch the latter, be contained by programmes or courses. Rather, thinking about management in the conceptual terms provided by the humanities and social sciences is a highly contagious matter, feeding back into strategic and governance issues: teaching students to question arguments whose validity has been taken for granted about their inherent frameworks of value, to question time-honoured organisational structures about the historical, political and social agenda behind them and to challenge assumptions about causality and derivation, impacts on those who are teaching and, through them, on academia as such. Business schools engaging with the humanities and social sciences in transformative management education, therefore, are faced with not only committing to transforming students but also committing to transforming themselves.

5

CONCLUSION

A Business Schools' Guide to the Galaxy of Transformative Management Education

42. This, according to Douglas Adams's famous science fiction comedy *The Hitch-hiker's Guide to the Galaxy*, is the answer to the question of all questions, an answer which Adams's protagonist Arthur Dent has diligently pursued throughout all his travels until he is presented with this number by the computer of all computers (Adams, 1979). Then his search starts again, this time the search for the question itself, while Earth, itself a wholesale computer simulation run by a network of computers, is about to be cancelled to make way for an intergalactic highway. In a rather similar manner, at the end of our report we find ourselves in a situation where, having collected so much material from which to draw conclusions on the future of management education, we have to ask exactly which question or questions are being answered by both our material and our conclusions from it. Of course we know which questions we asked during our interviews, but in hindsight, underlying both them and the answers we received there seems to appear a question which transcends the issue of how to provide transformative management education by integrating the humanities and social sciences—a question which perhaps might be answered by looking through the following lens: what is wrong in the relationship between academic business schools (and by extension, academia as a whole) and society that needs to be rectified by the reinvention of management education?

Let us sum up for one last time what we have found and subsequently deduced from our findings. Business schools which actively and determinedly work on the integration of the humanities and social sciences into management education, with a view to shifting it towards a more transformative approach to education, face a number of problems, as this is an approach which, at least at European universities, is not yet part of the academic mainstream. Those problems are due partly to an ingrained view of education as the imparting of instrumental information to an audience rather than engaging with students as persons, partly to the historically grown habit of disciplinary segregation with its ontological notion of knowledge and partly to the complexity of change management in an institutional setting where the academic privilege of the freedom of teaching and research makes even defining, much less enforcing common corporate principles of education rather difficult internally, while external stakeholders find it equally difficult to relate positively to academia and especially to academic business schools.

The problems we have outlined in our previous chapters can be solved, either by the measures we have suggested or by others which have not appeared to us, but to a certain extent they are secondary phenomena or, to put it differently, symptoms rather than causes of a more fundamental problem in the relationship between society and academia. This problem goes much further than the operational discomfort of managing the integration of the humanities and social sciences into transformative management education. The criticism recently directed at business schools was fuelled by the growing public understanding of a certain structural dysfunction, that is, shortcomings in the economic system of self-interest, the profit motive and the optimisation of personal gain. Capitalism has turned the global north into "externalization societies" based on imperial power structures (Lessenich, 2016, p. 107). Following growth imperatives in competitive markets has led to practices of ecological discharge which increase the environmental costs of value creation chains to the global south, constantly having to provide for "cheap nature" (Moore, 2016) to be exploited. "Living beyond the means of others"—as Lessenich (2016) poignantly reverses the well-known idiom—produces severe damage to ecological systems, as has become well known through the climate change debate and discussions on the end of carbon capitalism (Wallerstein et al., 2013).

Worst of all, such living creates an almost incredible asymmetry in the distribution of global wealth in which a fictitious 'Dogland'—a country built exclusively on the expenses devoted to dogs by their owners in the USA—would range in the mid-field of global incomes, US dogs being better off than 40% of the world human population (Korzeniewicz & Moran, 2009; Korzeniewicz, 2011). In Europe, the study by Thomas Piketty (2014) raised a debate on the liberal myths of merit-based participation, as his results clearly showed that an individual's life-time work performance could never come up with capital-generated revenues. Coinciding with reforms of pension systems which threaten seriously to lower the pensions of the now-working generations in many countries, even the global north's comparatively well-paid earners have realised in the meantime that this development affects them, accordingly reacting much more sensitively to such debates today than was the case in the last century. The protests following the financial crisis in 2008, most prominently the "We Are the 99%" campaigns, incarnated much of this critical spirit and made it globally visible, leading to much outspoken rage against the business schools which had educated the miscreants.

That both the public's growing awareness of the consequences of neo-liberal business practices and the global financial crises should lead to severe judgement on business schools' failure to prevent this by educating their students better is understandable. Moreover, this is one instance where the global standardisation of management education proved unfortunate, since it offered a handle with which to disparage business schools as a species, making this judgement generally hard to counter. That, however, the public should view business schools as being responsible for the way in which their graduates used the skills they were taught in their professional lives gives pause for thought, since it indicates that the public today expects business schools to train students in a way that imparts much more than mere managerial skills. Such skills, it seems, are understood as being amoral in nature, mere tools which in themselves offer no resistance to being misused. Worse, business schools today seem generally to be suspected of teaching concepts of management which, when followed through successfully, invite such misuse by claiming the merits of disinterested academic rigour for their practical application, thus condoning serious damage to the interests of society as a whole on the grounds that, if a procedure has been vetted and approved of academically, it is considered sound regardless of its possible detrimental consequences to the rest of the world.

Lying at the bottom of much of the criticism launched against business schools, this image hints at not only business schools but also academic education as such having effectively lost the trust of the public. As we have shown in our first chapter, this loss of trust is neither a recent phenomenon nor directly linked to business schools. When C. P. Snow in his famous Rede Lecture in 1959 accused academic scholars of being comprehensively divorced from reality, having been enabled by academic institutions to retreat intellectually as well as morally into the proverbial ivory tower (Snow, 1959), much of the damage haunting academic education today had already been done—not least by what was then the still-recent launching of atomic bombs at the end of World War Two, which had been made possible by scientists satisfying their intellectual curiosity about atomic fission without any apparent thought for the possible practical consequences of their research. Seen in this context, it is not so much business schools' future which is at stake in our current debate about management education but the future of academic education as such, since behind the attacks against business schools engendered by the financial crises lies the sneaking general suspicion that academics might tend to take advantage of the privilege of the freedom of teaching and research granted to them institutionally for their own rather than for society's benefit.

The fact that management education has received so much targeted criticism clearly has to do with the fact that, as the authors of the Carnegie report from 2011 stated in their very first sentence, "business has never mattered more" (Colby et al., 2011, p. 1). More perhaps than with most other educational endeavours, the effects of management education are more or less omnipresent in today's globalised world, as they are not at all limited to a clear-cut peer group of professionals or to one particular stratum of society closed off from other strata. Rather, as the crises of recent decades have spectacularly shown, what management students do after graduation directly or indirectly affects the whole of society and thus has the potential to do both great good as well as catastrophic damage to it, a potential that has become even more significant in the process of globalisation. Considering the way in which management and business expertise today is needed and employed in just about any kind of societal activity, the power that comes with this omnipresence is immense. In consequence, management education is a high-risk enterprise carrying an enormous burden of responsibility.

Business schools are aware of this responsibility. "Business schools are one of the most influential institutions in contemporary society, and have a particular role to play in setting high ethical standards for trust and fairness", as Mette Morsing from CBS and Alfons Sauquet Rovira from ESADE wrote in their Prologue to *Business Schools and Their Contribution to Society* (Morsing & Sauquet Rovira, 2011, p. XVIII). There is a dimension to this statement which bears further reflection: maintaining that such standards evidently need to be actively set, instead of being understood as an intrinsic part of academic education today, bears testimony to the erosion of confidence in universities' moral integrity not only on the part of society but also, to some extent, inside academia itself. This means that a crucial part of Wilhelm von Humboldt's notion of *Bildung*—the part, in fact, which embodied the ties between society and academia—has indeed been lost.

It was not or not primarily to benefit scholars themselves that Humboldt codified the freedom of teaching and research as the mainstay of the modern university's institutional identity; rather, its codification was the key part of a conceptual work which aimed at shaping the new institution into an agent of service to society as a whole. Put in charge of re-organising the Prussian university system as part of the national reforms after Prussia had been defeated by Napoleon, Humboldt designed his university with a view to freeing it from any other constraints but those immanent to pursuing "the pure idea of science itself" (Humboldt, 2010, pp. 255–56). Thus, on the face of it, while clearing the newly founded university prototype in Berlin from all suspicions of serving any political, economic or even religious agenda, the idea behind this of course was at the same time political in itself, as it stipulated the academic right to seek for knowledge for its own sake, regardless of its practical applicability. Since Napoleon had closed down several Prussian universities during the time of the French occupation, because he justly feared both scholars' and students' subversive influence on a population already chafing under the indignity of being reigned by the French enemy, the founding of the Berlin prototype was an act of defiance based on the Enlightenment movement's notion that all free thought was intrinsically rational and that furthermore rationality was intrinsically moral, which meant that the pursuit of knowledge for its own sake could not help but produce a value that would feed directly back into the development of an intrinsically moral society.

In the light of this concept of education, it seems that adopting transformation theory to reinvent management education is the obvious choice for meeting the challenge of (re-)setting the standards mentioned by Morsing and Sauquet

Rovira (2011). Jack Mezirow himself made it clear that he saw his theory being very much in line with the ideals that Humboldt had brought to the modern university:

> This theory is derived from cultural specific conditions associated with democratic societies and with the development of adult education as a vocation in Western Europe and North America, a liberal tradition that depends ultimately on faith in informed, free human choice and social justice. Rationality, self-awareness, and empathy are assumed values. Transformation Theory shares the normative goals of the Enlightenment of self-emancipation through self-understanding, the overcoming of systematically distorted communication, and the strengthening of the capacity for self-determination through rational discourse.
>
> *(Mezirow et al., 2000, p. XIV)*

Though Mezirow was usually wary of giving an explicit political spin to his theory, this passage hints at what might be perceived as a critical evaluation of the contemporary *status quo* not only of education but also of a society in which self-understanding is becoming increasingly scarce, systematically distorted communication is an accepted means of manipulating the public, and the link between rationality and self-determination is in danger of becoming extinct. Without saying so directly, Mezirow, like Humboldt, works on the assumption that rationality is intrinsically moral. Moreover, and here he is much more determined than Humboldt ever was, rationality is something which is essentially communicative, something which can only be experienced fully—and thus transformatively—in communication with others, a characteristic to which today's reality, in his eyes, is not congenial: "Our culture conspires against collaborative thinking and the development of social competence by conditioning us to think adversarially in terms of winning or losing, of proving ourselves smart, worthy, or wise" (Mezirow et al., 2000, p. 11).

Applied to the integration of the humanities and social sciences into transformative management education, the earlier passage could have been written expressly to describe the habit of mind induced by the tradition of the disciplinary segregation of knowledge. To be able to practise transformative management education, business schools will to a certain extent have to apply transformation theory to themselves, reflecting on the assumptions about management that they bring to teaching, checking those assumptions against societal reality, reframing them where necessary and thus reaching a new kind of self-determination through rational reasoning. One aspect, and perhaps the most important one, which certainly needs reframing in the light of the material we presented in our previous chapters is the very concept of academic knowledge. As we have pointed out, it is not the nature of knowledge as such which is the problem in interdisciplinary education; rather, it is the essentialist mind-set with which this knowledge is researched and taught. And if it is this mind-set, as we are rather inclined to believe, which is responsible both for the societal image of business schools offering mere tool-boxes for self-optimisation and for students' preference for instrumental learning, then it is this mind-set which needs to be the primary object of reforming management education. When the disciplines working together on transformative management education are linked to each other by a rational discourse shaped by both the will and the mutual respect that are necessary for successful interdisciplinary knowledge transfer, this might well help significantly with rebuilding business schools' relationship with society, since it would show that scholars, instead of simply fending for themselves, are able to understand themselves and to act as parts of a whole towards a common good.

It is with this interlinking of different types of knowledge that the humanities and social sciences can offer their most important contribution to transformative management education, setting moral standards in the shape of standards of epistemological awareness. These disciplines do not, as some of the more shallow clichés about the humanities and social sciences in management education would have it, 'own' morality or even rationality in any way; they simply provide for the moral and rational literacy necessary for transformative processes of reflection, by supplying "*complementary contexts* for reasoning and cultural knowledge that are crucial to functioning at a high level in the enveloping society" (Everett & Page, 2013, p. 8). In supplying such contexts, these disciplines counteract the selective perception of reality which is one of the most problematic aspects of instrumental teaching and learning, as Martha Nussbaum has put it rather pointedly in a passionate plea for the continued existence of the humanities at US universities:

> [E]ducators for economic growth will do more than to ignore the arts. They will fear them. For a cultivated and developed sympathy is a particular enemy of obtuseness, and moral obtuseness is necessary to carry out programs of economic development that ignore inequality.
>
> *(2011, p. 23)*

The "moral obtuseness" that Nussbaum castigates is not restricted to economists, far from it; rather, it is a side effect of the specialisation hype that has grown out of the disciplinary system. To counteract such over-specialisation in others, the humanities and social sciences themselves will first have to become aware of their own particular brand of obtuseness. At the business schools we visited, most humanities and social science scholars had already taken the step of reframing their understanding of their discipline of provenance in terms of a collective educational endeavour. To establish the participation of such scholars in transformative management education sustainably and, incidentally, to provide ways out of seriously overcrowded and underfunded disciplinary academic labour markets for them, humanities and social science scholars will individually, as well as institutionally, have to open up towards the demands of business schools for their contribution. In other words, they will have to re-avail themselves of the role of the educational "connecting tissue"—a phrase used repeatedly in this context by our interviewees at SMU (interview, 2014)—which had originally been prescribed for them by Humboldt, a role which somehow has fallen out of their collective memory since then but could and should celebrate a come-back today.

To conclude, what's wrong in the relations between business schools and society is only partly a problem of business schools themselves. Rather, it is a problem of higher education relating to challenges of the twenty-first century, that is, the impact of technology, globalisation and sustainability issues on academic institutions. The impact of technology, especially the digital accessibility of information, renders informational teaching modes obsolete, calling for innovative formats like blended learning, flipped-classroom teaching and feedback-based, student-teacher learning partnerships which, in Europe at least, are only just beginning to emerge. Globalisation threatens to equalise academic institutions through standardisation, challenging them to square the circle of remaining up to the standard and at the same time claiming recognisable identities of their own. The growing awareness of the dangers incurred by the unscrupulous exploiting of limited natural resources feeds into the public's equally growing distrust of an academia which not only lets this happen but, in the case of business schools, is perceived even to promote it. Taken together with the habitual inflexibility of European universities' organisational structures, which usually makes reforms of any kind very hard work for all concerned, all these factors contribute to universities currently not being recognised by the public as true partners in furthering the common good.

There is, however, light on the horizon, encouraging us in our conviction that integrating the humanities and social sciences into transformative management education could indeed change the situation sketched earlier. Certainly, at first glance, taking into account the problems with which the schools we visited were struggling might lead one to believe that the prospects of such education developing into a sustainable matrix for business schools seem dire, seeing that both scholars and schools are still largely wont to go in for "independence and competitiveness instead of integration and collaboration" (LeClair, 2013, p. 261) in order to satisfy short-term demands usually linked to disciplinary specialisation. "However, deeper exploration reveals a different, more positive future", as Daniel LeClair has recently claimed, "Under the surface, higher education is changing in ways that could both encourage and enable the fusion of liberal learning and business education", since "[u]niversities and business schools have found that their stakeholders have more in common than in conflict when considered in the context of social purpose" (2013, p. 261). The criticism that business schools have had to endure over recent years has, as became apparent in the public's expectation of more than just the imparting of instrumental managerial skills from business schools, has set an agenda for the latter which is explicitly conducive to educational endeavours, including the humanities and social sciences: "Through the lens of social purpose, the integration of liberal learning and business education is seen not only as desirable, but it is also viewed as necessary in the emerging environment" (LeClair, 2013, p. 261).

That the business schools we visited have understood this agenda and have started to act on that understanding is both a mark of faith in the humanities' and social sciences' societal relevance and a commitment to working towards society's common good. Due to their being more exposed to—and more aware of—public pressure forcing them continuously to recalibrate their societal role than most other academic institutions and, as the overwhelming amount of recent literature on the development of management education shows, due to their being more than ready to meet the challenge of such a redefinition, they are currently one of the most important influencers of higher education's future development as such. If any academic institution can achieve this redefinition, it will be for these schools, as the educational force behind future managers' contributions to the global change management required by the economic, societal and cultural challenges of the twenty-first century, to lead the way into a future reframed by the inclusion of the humanities and social sciences in transformative management education.

6

CODA

So Long, and Thanks for All the Fish

So Long, and Thanks for All the Fish is the title of the fourth book in Douglas Adams's series *The Hitchhiker's Guide to the Galaxy*, quoting the dolphins' final message to Earth as they leave it before its destruction to make way for a hyperspace by-pass. Although we have repeatedly maintained that the academic landscape of today seems to us to be under massive threat, we do not seriously consider it to be like a planet that is about to be wiped out. Rather, we draw a metaphorical parallel between Adams's Earth and our research project: like Adams's Earth, the work that we are rounding off with this Coda was programmed to achieve a certain goal, i.e. to describe best practices of involving the humanities and social sciences in management education and to draw some conclusions from such involvement, and the project was accordingly set up for a foreseeable life cycle, now, we hope, making way for a by-pass into the future of management education.

Having said this, we are also taking on the role of Adams's dolphins and would thus like to thank all of those who have so abundantly plied us with the fish making up our material. Thanks are due first and foremost to all our interviewees at CBS, ESADE, Koç, LUMS, SSE, HSG, Aalto and SMU, who answered all our questions so patiently and openly and thus helped us to showcase what magnificent work is done at their institutions; it was a huge pleasure meeting you. We apologise that we could not quote all of those who contributed, as our book would have grown in length out of all proportion, but to those who do not find their names in it, rest assured that each and every one of you has left your traces (even if invisible) in its fabric. And to those of you who have been quoted, we apologise if we have misunderstood or misrepresented you in any way; should this be the case, the fault is all ours.

A big warm thank you also goes to all the administrative staff of the schools we visited, who made our visits into such enjoyable occasions; you were so kind and attentive that we always came home humbly grateful for all that you did for us. Equally warmly we thank the Aspen Undergraduate Consortium, which repeatedly gave us the opportunity to present our work over recent years and to receive much invaluable input on it. To Bill Sullivan and to Matt Statler, who contributed the Foreword and the Afterword to our book, respectively, within an impossibly short time-frame, another huge thank you; you are stars! And last but not least, we profusely thank the Presidency of the University of St. Gallen, especially President Thomas Bieger, for so generously funding the project and thus making the writing of this book possible.

AFTERWORD

Matt Statler

Scholars and educators seeking to reinvent and transform management education will receive this book with delight and admiration. For the past decade, in anticipation of and in response to the publication of *Rethinking Undergraduate Business Education* (Colby et al., 2011), a paradigm shift has been taking shape and spreading across the global business school community. The factors contributing to this shift include an awareness of the practical limits of science as an approach to management, a sense of alarm about the series of scandals and crises that continues to unfold within markets and organisations and a desire to focus the power of business on the social and environmental challenges confronting people around the world.

The 2011 Carnegie report surveyed the field in the US, identified elements of a new paradigm and sketched out a practical path forward. Since that time, hundreds if not thousands of people have convened in various forums to discuss the integration of liberal learning within management education, and the paradigm has become more clearly defined to include the creative and performing arts as well as a greater variety of approaches to the humanities and social sciences as such. In particular, we have explored different ontologies of the 'human', epistemologies associated with 'practical reasoning', ethics appropriate to business practice in a volatile and uncertain world and aesthetics of discernment, judgement and creativity regarding what we imagine to be real.

As this book appears in print, the journals *Management Learning* and the *Academy of Management Learning and Education* have published calls for papers that further interrogate human rationality, while the prospect of major societal disruption associated with artificial intelligence and machine learning looms on the horizon. In such a context, this book presents a rich and nuanced source of educational practices that have developed within eight different business schools. My hope is that that these examples will inspire careful reflection as well as fearless innovation across the field and that thereby we can collectively contribute to the development of a more ethical and sustainable approach to management education and business practice.

APPENDIX

Panorama of Cases in Fact Sheets

Interview dates given in the text are those of the years of the site visits, as detailed next, unless otherwise indicated. The names of all interviewees are given in alphabetical order for each institution, with those not quoted in the text in square brackets. Student interviewees are mentioned at the end of each entry; the last names of student interviewees are withheld in order to preserve their anonymity.

Aalto University School of Business (Aalto), http://biz.aalto.fi/en/	Site visit: March 2015
Year of establishment	1911, as Helsinki School of Economics; now Aalto University School of Business
Stand-alone business school/ university or embedded in a multi-faculty university	Started as a stand-alone business school (public university); in 2010, merged with Helsinki University of Technology and University of Art and Design to form Aalto University
Predominant funding structure / ownership (public-private)	Part of private foundation-based, not-for-profit university (for sources and uses of funds, see www.aalto.fi/en/about/reports_ and_statistics/)
Total number of full-time academic staff	90
Total number of students	2,700 (see http://biz.aalto.fi/en/about/ avaintietoa/)
Number of degree programmes at bachelor, master, PhD and executive levels	BA: 13 MA: 25 PhD: 4

Aalto University School of Business (Aalto), http://biz.aalto.fi/en/	Site visit: March 2015
Humanities and social sciences: definition	N/A
Staff employed as percentage of total full-time academic staff	N/A
Level of integration (university-programme-course)	Humanities and social sciences as such not being integrated into management education, because these disciplines are part of another university; interdisciplinary co-operation being fostered between management and design studies
People interviewed, their academic titles and roles	[Ingmar Björkman, Professor of Management and Dean, School of Business] [Minna Halme, Professor, Department of Management Studies] **Seppo Ikäheimo**, Professor of Finance and Accounting and Vice-Dean, School of Business [Annukka Jyrämä, Research and Innovation Services] **Mikko Koria**, Professor of Practice, Department of Management Studies **Tuija Nikko**, Quality Manager, Dean's Unit, School of Business [Fernando Pinto Santos, Postdoctoral Researcher, Department of Management Studies] [Armi Temmes, Professor of Practice, Department of Management Studies] [Christa Uusi-Rauva, Dr., Lecturer, Department of Management Studies]

Copenhagen Business School (CBS), www.cbs.dk/en	Site visit: October 2014
Year of establishment	1917; integrated as an institution of higher education into the Danish education system in 1965
Stand-alone business school/ university or embedded in a multi-faculty university	Stand-alone business school
Predominant funding structure/ ownership (public-private)	Public

Copenhagen Business School (CBS), www.cbs.dk/en	Site visit: October 2014
Total number of full-time academic staff	561
Total number of students	22,564
Number of degree programmes at Bachelor, Master, PhD and executive levels	BA: 20 MA: 22 PhD: various research fields offered at three doctoral schools Part- and full-time programmes in continuing education: 12
Humanities and Social Sciences: definition	Department of Management, Politics and Philosophy (MPP)
Staff employed as percentage of total full-time academic staff	63 / 561 = 11%
Level of integration (university-programme-course)	Programme level, run by the MPP
People interviewed, their academic titles and roles	**Edward Ashbee**, Professor, Programme Director, Sociology and Management **Sven Bislev**, Associate Professor, Vice-Dean of Education [Martin Jes Iversen, Associate Professor, Programme Director, BSc International Shipping and Trade] **Rasmus Johnsen**, Associate Professor, Department of Management, Politics and Philosophy **Sine N. Just**, Associate Professor, Programme Director, Sociology and Management, Department of Business and Politics **Annemette Kjærgaard**, Associate Professor, Vice-Dean of Learning **Kristian Kreiner**, Professor, Director of Centre for Management Studies of the Building Process **Jan Molin**, Dean of Education [Annette Risberg, Associate Professor, Programme Director, Business Language and Culture, Department of Intercultural Communication and Management] **Dorte Salskov-Iversen**, Vice-President and Head, Department of Intercultural Communication and Management

Copenhagen Business School (CBS), www.cbs.dk/en	Site visit: October 2014
	[Lene Mette Sørensen, Director of Principles for Responsible Management Education and Sustainability Office, Department of Intercultural Communication and Management]
	[Morten Sørensen Thaning, Associate Professor, Department of Management, Politics and Philosophy]
	Maiken, **Katrin** and **Helene**, students

ESADE, Barcelona (ESADE), www.esade.edu/en/	Site visit: January 2015
Year of establishment	1958
Stand-alone business school/ university or embedded in a multi-faculty university	Stand-alone business school
Predominant funding structure/ ownership (public-private)	Private
Total number of full-time academic staff	213 (Business School)
Total number of students	Business School: 2,046 Law School: 1,215 Executive Education: 7,776
Number of degree programmes at Bachelor, Master, PhD and executive levels	BA: 4 MA: 5 PhD: 3 Executive: 7
Humanities and Social Sciences: definition **Staff employed as percentage of total full-time academic staff**	Department of Social Sciences 12 / 214 = 5.6%
Level of integration (university-programme-course)	Programme level: BBA flagship
People interviewed, their academic titles and roles	**Daniel Arenas Vives**, Associate Professor and Director, Department of Social Sciences **Eduard Bonet Guinó**, Professor Emeritus, Department of Strategy and General Management

ESADE, Barcelona (ESADE), www.esade.edu/en/	Site visit: January 2015
	Anna Iñesta, Dr., Director, Center for Educational Innovation
	Josep M. Lozano, Professor of Business Ethics and Corporate Social Responsibility, Department of Social Sciences
	Joan Rodón Mòdol, Associate Professor, Department of Operations, Innovation and Data Sciences
	[Josep M. Sayeras Maspera, Associate Professor and Associate Dean, Department of Economics, Finance and Accounting]

Koç University, Istanbul (Koç), www.ku.edu.tr/en	Site visit: November 2014
Year of establishment	1993
Stand-alone business school/ university or embedded in a multi-faculty university	Started as a business school, but has extended its scope to include law, medicine, information technology and engineering
Predominant funding structure/ ownership (public-private)	Private
Total number of full-time academic staff	823
Total number of students	5,300 (200 being enrolled in the graduate business school)
Number of degree programmes at Bachelor, Master, PhD and executive levels	BA: 26 MA: 31 PhD: 25
Humanities and Social Sciences: definition	College of Social Sciences and Humanities; Graduate School of Social Sciences and Humanities
Staff employed as percentage of total full-time academic staff	N/A
Level of integration (university-programme-course)	University level
People interviewed, their academic titles and roles	**Ali Çarkoğlu**, Professor and Dean of undergraduate education
	Zeynep Gürhan Canlı, Professor and Associate Dean for graduate programmes in Business
	Ümran İnan, Professor, President

Koç University, Istanbul (Koç), www.ku.edu.tr/en	Site visit: November 2014
	[Özge Pala, Assistant Professor, Organisational Behaviour] [Charilaos Platanakis, Assistant Professor, Philosophy] [Scott Withrow, Assistant Professor, Psychometrics]

Lancaster University Management School (LUMS), www.lancaster.ac.uk/lums/	Site visit: March 2015
Year of establishment	1964
Stand-alone business school/ university or embedded in a multi-faculty university	Business school embedded in multi-faculty university Lancaster University comprises four faculties: Management School (LUMS) School of Arts and Social Sciences School of Medicine and Health School of Science and Technology
Predominant funding structure/ ownership (public-private)	Public
Total number of full-time academic staff	337
Total number of students	3,765
Number of degree programmes at Bachelor, Master, PhD and executive levels	BA: 62 MA: 27 PhD: 7
Humanities and Social Sciences: definition	Department of Organisation, Work and Technology
Staff employed as percentage of total full-time academic staff	30 / 337 = 8.9%
Level of integration (university-programme-course)	Programme level: BBA in Management Studies and European Languages
People interviewed, their academic titles and roles	[Kostas Amiridis, Dr., Lecturer] **Bogdan Costea**, Professor **Sue Cox**, Professor, Dean Emerita, Vice-President of EFMD [Robert Geyer, Professor of Politics, Complexity and Policy]

Lancaster University Management School (LUMS), www.lancaster.ac. uk/lums/	Site visit: March 2015
	Laurence Hemming, Professor of Philosophy **Lucas Introna**, Professor of Information Technology **Cecile Rozuel**, Dr., Teaching Fellow [Pete Thomas, Senior Lecturer and Programme Director, MSc Human Resource and Knowledge Management and MSc Politics, Philosophy and Management] **Theodore Vurdubakis**, Professor and Head, Department of Organisation, Work and Technology

Singapore Management University (SMU), www.smu.edu.sg/	Site visit: September 2014
Year of establishment	2000
Stand-alone business school/ university or embedded in a multi-faculty university	Stand-alone business university
Predominant funding structure/ ownership (public-private)	Public
Total number of full-time academic staff	447
Total number of students	7,791 full-time undergraduates 1,489 full-time and part-time postgraduates
Number of degree programmes at Bachelor, Master, PhD and executive levels	BA: 7 MA: 22 PhD: 9 Graduate diploma: 2 Executive: 2
Humanities and Social Sciences: definition	School of Social Sciences 44 / 447 = 9.8%
Staff employed as percentage of total full-time academic staff	
Level of integration (university-programme-course)	Course level, within School of Social Sciences; courses offered in the *University Core* section as well as through the *Arts Management* major

Singapore Management University (SMU), www.smu.edu.sg/	Site visit: September 2014
People interviewed, their academic titles and roles	**Francis Koh**, Professor of Financial Management, Head of Special Projects **Sriven Naidu,** Head of Strategic Planning **Yang Hoong Pang**, Professor and Vice-Provost of undergraduate education, Dean of School of Accountancy **Yeing Soh**, Head, Office of Dean of Students Group Services **James Tang**, Professor and Dean, School of Social Sciences, Chair of "humanities@ smu" task force

Stockholm School of Economics (SSE), www.hhs.se/	Site visit: March 2015
Year of establishment	1909
Stand-alone business school/ university or embedded in a multi-faculty university	Stand-alone business school
Predominant funding structure/ ownership (public-private)	Independent private institution funded by the Swedish business community; not regulated by the Higher Education Ordinance
Total number of full-time academic staff	147
Total number of students	1,800 (see www.hhs.se/globalassets/ blocks-do-not-edit/printed-matter/ factsheets/fact_sheet_general.pdf)
Number of degree programmes at Bachelor, Master, PhD and executive levels	BSc: 3 MSc: 5 PhD: 3 Executive MBA: 4
Humanities and Social Sciences: definition	Department of Law, Language and Economic Statistics
Staff employed as percentage of total full-time academic staff	15 / 147 = 8.2%
Level of integration (university-programme-course)	At a formal level, no integration taking place: humanities scholars scarce; integration not planned, core being emphasised
People interviewed, their academic titles and roles	**Jesper Blomberg**, Associate Professor, Department of Management and Organization

Stockholm School of Economics (SSE), www.hhs.se/	Site visit: March 2015
	[Kajsa Fung, Director, Quality Assurance] [Per Henrik Hedberg, Research Fellow] **Thomas Lavelle**, Lecturer, Department of Law, Languages and Economic Statistics, and Director, Center for Modern Languages [Lars-Olof Lychnell, Research Fellow, Department of Management and Organization] **Anthony Magistrale**, Professor, The Swedish Program [Alan Shima, Lecturer] **Emma Stenström**, Associate Professor, Department of Management and Organization [Lars Strannegård, Professor, Department of Management and Organization, President] [Karin Svedberg Helgesson, Associate Professor, Department of Management and Organization] [Anne von Bergen, Special Advisor, Quality Assurance] **Ken Wagner**, Founder and Director, The Swedish Program **Isak**, Student, Director of Art Initiative

University of St. Gallen (HSG), www.unisg.ch/	Site visit: May 2015
Year of establishment	1898
Stand-alone business school/ university or embedded in a multi-faculty university	Stand-alone business school
Predominant funding structure/ ownership (public-private)	Public
Total number of full-time academic staff	289
Total number of students	8,020
Number of degree programmes at Bachelor, Master, PhD and executive levels	BA: 5 MA: 20 PhD: 6 Executive: 8
Humanities and Social Sciences: definition Staff employed as percentage of total full-time academic staff	School of Humanities and Social Sciences 34 / 289 = 11.7%

University of St. Gallen (HSG), www.unisg.ch/	Site visit: May 2015
Level of integration (university-programme-course)	University level
People interviewed, their academic titles and roles	[Emmanuel Alloa, Assistant Professor of Cultural Theory and Philosophy] **Omid Ashari**, Professor and Programme Director, Master in Strategy and International Management, School of Management **Thomas Beschorner**, Professor and Director, Institute for Business Ethics **James W. Davis**, Professor and Director, Institute for Political Science **Martin J. Eppler**, Professor of Media and Communication Management **Dieter Euler**, Professor of Educational Management, School of Management **Simon Evenett**, Professor of International Trade and Economic Development [Lucas Gschwend, Professor and Dean, Law School] **Caspar Hirschi**, Professor of History [Martin Huser, Dr., Vice-President] **Vincent Kaufmann**, Professor of French and Director, Institute for Media and Communications Management [Markus Menz, Professor, Institute of Management] [Christoph Michels, Assistant Professor, Institute of Organisational Psychology] [Günter Müller-Stewens, Professor and Chair, Institute of Management] [Julia Nentwich, Associate Professor, Institute of Organisational Psychology] **Vito Roberto**, Professor of Law and Vice-President for Teaching **Kuno Schedler**, Professor of Public Management **Ulrich Schmid**, Professor of Russian Culture and Society [Florian Schulz, Dr., Head of Psychological Counselling Services] **Chris Steyaert**, Professor and Director, Institute of Organisational Psychology **Florian Wettstein**, Professor of Business Ethics **Dardan** and **Sarah**, Students

REFERENCES

AACSB. (2017). *Eligibility procedures and accreditation standards for business accreditation.* Tampa, FL: Association to Advance Collegiate Schools of Business.

Adams, D. (1979). *The hitchhiker's guide to the galaxy.* London: Pan Macmillan.

Adams, D. (1984). *So long, and thanks for all the fish.* London: Pan Macmillan.

Amdam, R. P., Kvålshaugen, R., & Larsen, E. (Eds.). (2003). *Inside the business schools: The content of European business education.* Copenhagen: Copenhagen Business School Press.

Augier, M., & March, J. G. (2011). *The roots, rituals, and rhetorics of change: North American business schools after the Second World War.* Stanford: Stanford Business Books.

Bachmann, G., & Shah, N. (2016). Hacking the classroom: Rethinking learning through social media practices. In C. Steyaert et al. (Eds.), *The Routledge companion to reinventing management education* (pp. 287–97). London: Routledge.

Bardecki, M. (2015). Developing and managing integrated (interdisciplinary/transdisciplinary) graduate programs in Environmental Science and Management in a collaborative context. In W. Leal Filho et al. (Eds.), *Integrative approaches to sustainable development at university level: Making the links* (pp. 197–209). Cham: Springer.

Benington, J., & Moore, M. H. (Eds.). (2011). *Public value: Theory and practice.* Basingstoke: Palgrave Macmillan.

Beveridge, T. S., Fruchter, L. L., Sanmartin, C. V., & deLottinville, C. B. (2013). Evaluating the use of reflective practice in a nonprofessional, undergraduate clinical communication skills course. *Teaching in Higher Education, 19*(1), 58–71.

Bickerstaffe, G. (2009). Towards Europe. *Global Focus: The EFMD Business Magazine, 3*(3), 8–12.

Bonet, E. (2015). *Educating managers for the twenty-first century.* Barcelona: ESADE.

Boud, D. (1999). Avoiding the traps: Seeking good practice in the use of self-assessment and reflection in professional courses. *Social Work Education, 18*(2), 121–32.

Boyd, R. (Ed.). (1991). *Personal transformation in small groups.* New York: Routledge.

Boyd, R., & Myers, J. (1988). Transformative education. *International Journal of Lifelong Education, 7*(4), 261–84.

Braidotti, R. (2013). *The posthuman.* Cambridge: Polity.

CBS. (2011). *CBS strategy: Business in society.* (unpublished, s.p.).

Colby, A., Ehrlich, T., Beaumont, E., & Stephens, J. (2003). *Educating citizens: Preparing America's undergraduates for lives of moral and civic responsibility.* San Francisco: Jossey-Bass.

Colby, A., Ehrlich, T., Sullivan, W. M., & Dolle, J. R. (2011). *Rethinking undergraduate business education: Liberal learning for the profession.* San Francisco: Jossey-Bass and the Carnegie Foundation for the Advancement of Teaching.

Cranton, P. (2006). Musings and reflections on the meaning, context and process of transformative learning: A dialogue between John M. Dirkx and Jack Mezirow. *Journal of Transformative Education, 4*(2), 123–39.

Cranton, P., & King, K. P. (2003). Transformative learning as a professional development goal. *New Directions for Adult and Continuing Education, 98*, 31–7.

Daloz, L. A. P. (2000). Transformative learning for the common good. In J. Mezirow (Ed.), *Learning as transformation: Critical perspectives on a theory in progress* (pp. 103–24). San Francisco: Jossey-Bass.

Davis, M. M. (2013). Challenges facing today's business schools. In G. M. Hardy & D. L. Everett (Eds.), *Shaping the future of business education: Relevance, rigor and life preparation* (pp. 26–39). New York: Palgrave Macmillan.

Derrida, J. (2002). The university without condition. In J. Derrida (Ed.), P. Kamuf (Trans.), *Without alibi* (pp. 202–37). Stanford: Stanford University Press.

Dewey, J. (1984). The quest for certainty: A study of the relation of knowledge and action. In J. A. Boydston (Ed.), *The later works, 1925–1953* (Vol. 4). Carbondale, IL: Southern Illinois University Press. (Original work published 1929).

Dilthey, W. (1989). Introduction to the human sciences. In R. A. Makkreel & F. Rodi (Eds.), *Selected works* (Vol. 1). Princeton, NJ: Princeton University Press.

Dirkx, J. M. (1998). Transformative learning theory in the practice of adult education: An overview. *PAACE Journal of Lifelong Learning, 7*, 1–14.

Dirkx, J. M. (2003). Authenticity and imagination. *New Directions for Adult and Continuing Education, 111*, 27–39.

Doidge, N. (2007). *The brain that changes itself: Stories of personal triumph from the frontiers of brain science.* New York: Viking.

Duke, S., & Appleton, J. (2000). The use of reflection in a palliative care programme: A quantitative study of the development of reflective skills over an academic year. *Journal of Advanced Nursing, 32*(6), 1557–68.

Dyment, J. E., & O'Connell, T. S. (2010). The quality of reflection in student journals: A review of limiting and enabling factors. *Innovative Higher Education, 35*(4), 233–44.

Dyment, J. E., & O'Connell, T. S. (2011). Assessing the quality of reflection in student journals: A review of the research. *Teaching in Higher Education, 16*(1), 81–97.

Eberle, T. S., & Metelmann, J. (2016). Integrating humanities and social sciences: Institutionalizing a contextual studies programme. In C. Steyaert et al. (Eds.), *The Routledge companion to reinventing management education* (pp. 398–414). London: Routledge.

ESADE. (2013). *Working group on improvements to the BBA curriculum: Conclusions and proposals.* Barcelona: ESADE. (unpublished, s.p.).

ESADE. (2015). *Working group on improvements to the BBA curriculum (II): Conclusions and proposals.* Barcelona: ESADE. (unpublished, s.p.).

von Eschenbach, Wolfram. (2004). *Parzival.* (C. Edwards, Trans.). Cambridge: Brewer.

Everett, L. D., & Page, M. J. (2013). The crucial educational fusion: Relevance, rigor, and life preparation in a changing world. In G. M. Hardy & D. L. Everett (Eds.), *Shaping the future of business education: Relevance, rigor and life preparation* (pp. 1–18). New York: Palgrave Macmillan.

Foucault, M. (1984). What is enlightenment? In P. Rabinow (Ed.), C. Porter (Trans.), *The Foucault reader* (pp. 32–50). New York: Pantheon.

Freire, P. (1970). *Pedagogy of the oppressed*. New York: Seabury Press.

Funda Yağcı Acar, H., Ergin, M., Emrah Oder, B., Karaesmen, F., & Yılmaz, K. *Report on the core programme revision* (Koç 2011, unpublished, s.p.).

Gordon, R. A., & Howell, J. E. (1959). *Higher education for business*. New York: Columbia University Press.

Habermas, J. (1971). *Knowledge and human interests*. (J. J. Shapiro, Trans.). Boston: Beacon.

Hardy, G. M., & Everett, D. L. (Eds.). (2013). *Shaping the future of business education: Relevance, rigor, and life preparation*. New York: Palgrave Macmillan.

Harney, S., & Thomas, H. (2013). Towards a liberal management education. *Journal of Management Development, 32*(5), 508–24.

Hedmo, T. (2004). *Rule-making in the transnational space: The development of European accreditation of management education* (Doctoral dissertation). Uppsala: Företagsekonomiska Institutionen.

Hirsch, E. D., Jr. (1987). *Cultural literacy: What every American needs to know*. Boston: Houghton Mifflin.

Humboldt, W. von. (2010). *Werke in fünf Bänden (Studienausgabe): Teil 4: Schriften zur Politik und zum Bildungswesen*. Darmstadt: Wissenschaftliche Buchgesellschaft.

HSG (1999/2000). https://shared.unisg.ch/sites/uniarchiv/Publikationsarchiv/Jahresbericht_1999-2000.pdf

Johnsen, R., Thaning, M. S., & Pedersen, M. (2016). Knowledge you can't Google: Teaching philosophy at the business school. In C. Steyaert et al. (Eds.), *The Routledge companion to reinventing management education* (pp. 374–86). London: Routledge.

Kegan, R. (1982). *The evolving self: Problem and process in human development*. Cambridge, MA: Harvard University Press.

Kegan, R. (2009). What 'form' transforms? A constructive-developmental approach to transformative learning. In K. Illeris (Ed.), *Contemporary theories of learning: Learning theorists in their own words* (pp. 35–52). London: Routledge.

Khurana, R. (2007). *From higher aims to hired hands: The social transformation of American business schools and the unfulfilled promise of management as a profession*. Princeton, NJ: Princeton University Press.

Kligyte, G. (2011). Transformation narratives in academic practice. *International Journal for Academic Development, 16*(3), 201–13.

Kohlberg, L. (1984). *The psychology of moral development: The nature and validity of moral stages*. New York: Harper & Collins.

Kolb, D. A. (1984). *Experiential learning: Experience as the source of learning and development*. Englewood Cliffs, NJ: Prentice-Hall.

Korzeniewicz, R. P. (2011). Inequality: On some of the implications of a world-historical perspective. *DesiguALdades.net Working Paper Series, 3*.

Korzeniewicz, R. P., & Moran, T. P. (2009). *Unveiling inequality: A world-historical perspective*. New York: Russell Sage Foundation.

Kvålshaugen, R. (2001). *The antecedents of management competence: The role of educational background and type of work experience* (Doctoral dissertation). Sandvika: Norwegian School of Management BI.

Landfester, U., Brenneche, N. T., & Prat-i-Pubill, Q. (2016). 'Humanities' Business' and other narratives: How to read the future of management education? In C. Steyaert et al. (Eds.), *The Routledge companion to reinventing management education* (pp. 49–64). London: Routledge.

Lange, O. (2009). The story of a business school, 1987–2009. In J. Molin & A. Irwin (Eds.), *The distinctiveness of diversity: CBS, a case in point* (pp. 23–36). Frederiksberg: Copenhagen Business School.

Leal Filho, W., Brandli, L., Kuznetskova, O., & Finisterra do Paço, A. M. (Eds.). (2015). *Integrative approaches to sustainable development at university level: Making the links.* Cham: Springer.

LeClair, D. R. (2013). Prospects for fusing liberal learning and business education in the changing environment of higher education. In G. M. Hardy & D. L. Everett (Eds.), *Shaping the future of business education: Relevance, rigor and life preparation* (pp. 252–62). New York: Palgrave Macmillan.

Lessenich, S. (2016). *Neben uns die Sintflut: Die Externalisierungsgesellschaft und ihr Preis.* Munich: Hanser.

Locke, R. R. (1989). *Management and higher education since 1940: The influence of America and Japan on Germany, Great Britain, and France.* Cambridge: Cambridge University Press.

Lysaker, J., & Furuness, S. (2011). Space for transformation: Relational, dialogic pedagogy. *Journal of Transformative Education, 9*(3), 183–97.

Malabou, C. (2011). The future of humanities. *Transeuropéennes: Revue internationale de pensée critique, 4*, 1–6. http://transeuropeennes.org/ar/articles/281/The_future_of_Humanities. html [26.09.2018]

Maloney, S., Tai, J. H-M., Lo, K., Molloy, E., & Ilic, D. (2013). Honesty in critically reflective essays: An analysis of student practice. *Advances in Health Sciences Education: Theory and Practice, 18*(4), 617–26.

Merck, J., & Beermann, M. (2015). The relevance of transdisciplinary teaching and learning for the successful integration of sustainability issues into higher education development. In W. Leal Filho et al. (Eds.), *Integrative approaches to sustainable development at university level: Making the links* (pp. 19–25). Cham: Springer.

Mezirow, J. (1978). *Education for perspective transformation: Women's re-entry programs in community colleges.* New York: Center for Adult Education, Teachers College, Columbia University.

Mezirow, J. (1981). A critical theory of adult learning and education. *Adult Education, 32*(1), 3–24.

Mezirow, J. (1991). *Transformative dimensions of adult learning.* San Francisco: Jossey-Bass.

Mezirow, J. (2009). An overview on transformative learning. In K. Illeris (Ed.), *Contemporary theories of learning: Learning theorists in their own words* (pp. 90–105). London: Routledge.

Mezirow, J. et al. (1990). *Fostering critical reflection in adulthood: A guide to transformative and emancipatory learning.* San Francisco: Jossey-Bass.

Mezirow, J. et al. (Eds.). (2000). *Learning as transformation: Critical perspectives on a theory in progress.* San Francisco: Jossey-Bass.

Miller, J. P., & Seller, W. (1985). *Curriculum: Perspectives and practice.* New York: Longman.

Miller, T. (2012). *Blow up the humanities.* Philadelphia: Temple University Press.

Mintzberg, H. (2004). *Managers not MBAs: A hard look at the soft practice of managing and management development.* San Francisco: Berrett-Koehler.

Moore, J. W. (2016). The rise of cheap nature. In J. W. Moore (Ed.), *Anthropocene or capitalocene?* (pp. 78–115). Oakland: PM Press.

Morsing, M., & Sauquet Rovira, A. (Eds.). (2011). *Business schools and their contribution to society.* London: Sage.

Namaste, N. B. (2017). Designing and evaluating students' transformative learning. *The Canadian Journal for the Scholarship of Teaching and Learning, 8*(3).

Nussbaum, M. (2011). *Not for profit: Why democracy needs the humanities.* Princeton, NJ: Princeton University Press.

O'Connor, E. S. (2012). *Creating new knowledge in management: Appropriating the field's lost foundations.* Stanford: Stanford Business Books.

O'Connor, E. S. (2016). The test of time: Historical perspectives on management education reform in the US. In C. Steyaert et al. (Eds.), *The Routledge companion to reinventing management education* (pp. 36–48). London: Routledge.

Östling, J. (2018). *Humboldt and the modern German university: An intellectual history.* (L. Olsson, Trans.). Lund: Lund University Press.

Parker, M. (2016). Organization and philosophy: Vision and division. In R. Mir et al. (Eds.), *The Routledge companion to philosophy in organization studies* (pp. 491–98). London: Routledge.

Pascarella, E. T., & Terenzini, P. T. (2005). *How college affects students: A third decade of research* (Vol. 2). San Francisco: Jossey-Bass.

Pickering, A. (1992). From science as knowledge to science as practice. In A. Pickering (Ed.), *Science as practice and culture* (pp. 1–26). Chicago: University of Chicago Press.

Piketty, T. (2014). *Capital in the twenty-first century.* (A. Goldhammer, Trans.). Cambridge, MA: Harvard University Press.

Platzer, H., Blake, D., & Ashford, D. (2000). Barriers to learning from reflection: A study of the use of groupwork with post-registration nurses. *Journal of Advanced Nursing, 31*(5), 1001–08.

Raffnsøe, S. (2013). *The human turn: The makings of a contemporary relational topography.* Frederiksberg: Copenhagen Business School.

Rüegg-Stürm, J., & Grand, S. (2015). *The St. Gallen management model.* Bern: Haupt Verlag.

Scharmer, C. O. (2016). *Theory U: Leading from the future as it emerges* (2nd ed.). San Francisco: Berrett-Koehler.

Schön, D. A. (1983). *The reflective practitioner: How professionals think in action.* New York: Basic Books.

Schön, D. A. (1992). The theory of inquiry: Dewey's legacy to education. *Curriculum Inquiry, 22*(2), 119-39.

Segal, N. et al. (2013). *Cultural literacy in Europe today.* Strasbourg: European Science Foundation.

Shapin, S. (2012). The ivory tower: The history of a figure of speech and its cultural uses. *British Journal for the History of Science, 45*(1), 1–27.

Snow, C. P. (1959). *The two cultures and the scientific revolution.* Cambridge: Cambridge University Press.

Starkey, K., & Tempest, S. (2008). A clear sense of purpose? The evolving role of the business school. *Journal of Management Development, 27*(4), 379–90.

Starkey, K., & Tiratsoo, N. (2007). *The business school and the bottom line.* Cambridge: Cambridge University Press.

Statler, M., & Salovaara, P. (2016). Thinking in and of the world: Actualizing wisdom and pragmatism in business education? In C. Steyaert et al. (Eds.), *The Routledge companion to reinventing management education* (pp. 206–20). London: Routledge.

Steyaert, C., Beyes, T., & Parker, M. (Eds.). (2016). *The Routledge companion to reinventing management education.* London: Routledge.

Taylor, E. (1998). *The theory and practice of transformative learning: A critical review* (Information Series, 374). Columbus: ERIC Clearinghouse on Adult, Career, and Vocational Education.

Thomä, D. (2005). Drei Prinzipien und drei Phasen der 'Humboldt-Kultur': Erfindung, Krise und ein Leben nach dem Tod. In S. Spoun & W. Wunderlich (Eds.), *Studienziel Persönlichkeit: Beiträge zum Bildungsauftrag der Universität heute* (pp. 49–70). Frankfurt: Campus.

Thomas, H., Lee, M., Thomas, L., & Wilson, A. (Eds.). (2014). *Securing the future of management education: Competitive destruction or constructive innovation?* (Vol. 2). Bedfordshire: Emerald Group.

Ulrich, H., & Krieg, W. (1972). *Das St. Galler Management-Modell.* Bern: Haupt Verlag.

Wade, R. C., & Yarbrough, D. B. (1996). Portfolios: A tool for reflective thinking in teacher education? *Teaching and Teacher Education, 12*(1), 63–79.

Wallerstein, I. et al. (2013). *Does capitalism have a future?* New York: Oxford University Press.

Weller Swanson, K. (2010). Constructing a learning partnership in transformative teacher development. *Reflective Practice, 11*(2), 259–69.

White, H. (1987). *The content of the form: Narrative discourse and historical representation.* Baltimore: Johns Hopkins University Press.

White, R. M. (2015). Who am I? The role(s) of an academic at a 'sustainable' university. In W. Leal Filho et al. (Eds.), *Integrative approaches to sustainable development at university level: Making the links* (pp. 675–86). Cham: Springer.

Winterson, J. (1989). *Sexing the cherry.* London: Bloomsbury.

INDEX

Note: Page numbers in italic indicate a figure on the corresponding page.